The Terror of Existence

From Ecclesiastes to Theatre of the Absurd

GW00566796

The Terror of Existence

From Ecclesiastes to Theatre of the Absurd

Theodore Dalrymple & Kenneth Francis

Published by New English Review Press
a subsidiary of World Encounter Institute
PO Box 158397
Nashville, Tennessee 37215
&
27 Old Gloucester Street
London, England, WC1N 3AX

Cover Art and Design by Kendra Mallock

ISBN: 978-1-943003-22-8

First Edition

NEW ENGLISH REVIEW PRESS
newenglishreview.org

For my Mother

—**Kenneth Francis**

Contents

'For what shall it profit a man, if he shall gain the whole world, and lose his own soul?' (Mark 8:36)

Acknowledgments

We should like to thank our publisher and editor Rebecca Bynum most sincerely for having taken on this unusual book. We are deeply in her debt. We would also like to thank designer Kendra Mallock for the book's artwork.

Both authors would like to thank each other for a pleasant and frictionless co-operation. Although we have corresponded often by e-mail, we have met only once, in a Dublin pub, but look forward to more such meetings.

Theodore Dalrymple
Kenneth Francis

Introduction
Theodore Dalrymple

No one, I suspect, goes more than a few minutes, at most, without making a judgment either aesthetic or moral. I do not mean by this that practically everyone spends much of his waking time reflecting deeply on, and consciously puzzling over, questions of taste and ethics. But he makes judgments of this kind nonetheless, even if he does not make them explicit to himself.

On the contrary, aesthetic and moral judgment is so inextricably entwined in human thought itself that most of us, most of the time, do not even realise that we are making such judgments. When I go into my garden when it is in flower, for example, I do not enumerate its characteristics and conclude, as with a syllogism, that it is beautiful. My apprehension of its beauty is virtually simultaneous with my perception: but that does not mean that it is not a judgment.

Indeed, it is scarcely possible to imagine human beings who made no aesthetic or moral judgments. What would they be like? It is easy enough to imagine people with very different scales of values from our own – indeed, we meet such people every day – but we never meet anyone with no scale of values, even if his scale is repellent to us or is inconsistent from moment to moment. *The Mountain People* was a famous book by the social anthropologist, Colin Turnbull, who described a Ugandan tribe called the Ik whose members, after their eviction from their ancestral lands and the consequent loss of traditional way of life, became to all appearances utterly amoral. According to Turnbull's account, they ceased to care for one another, behaved with extreme callousness or cruelty to those among them who were suffering, including their own parents and children, and remorselessly preyed on one another, taking advantage of every situation in the most blatantly egotistical way imaginable. The accuracy of Turnbull's account has been disputed (he is said not to have spoken the Ik language, and was thought by others to have misunderstood everything that he witnessed), but even if his account were a true one, that the Ik were precisely as he portrayed them, namely as a collection of psychopaths, it would not be true that, individually, they had no scale of values. The problem was that they had become so atomised that their own survival was the only thing that mattered to them – but it did matter.

I take it, then, that our very constitution as human beings, and our situation as social animals, entails, or imposes the necessity on us of making judgments. These days, one sometimes hears people praise themselves for being non-judgmental, but this is a misuse of language. What they mean is that they are not, or at least do not consider themselves to be, censorious, that is to say the kind of person who makes quick and damning judgments on others (actually, they are very likely to be censorious towards those whom they consider censorious). They cannot possibly mean that they do not make judgments, because the supposed desirability of not making judgments is itself a judgment. You would have to be very imperfectly conscious to make no judgment. Judgments are like conventions: you can change them, but you cannot escape them.

Though we are forced by our existential position, so to speak, to make judgments, the metaphysical basis on which we make them is for most of us uncertain. Moreover, the very of people who consider the question of the metaphysical basis of judgment has increased enormously with the spread of tertiary education. People who might once have accepted the moral and aesthetic judgments of others, or those that were handed down to them in religious teaching, and who had neither the time nor the leisure to examine them, now demand full and indubitable justifications for any and all judgments. If no such justifications can be found, if in fact there is no Cartesian point from which such judgments can be levered, moral and aesthetic cacophony is bound to follow: to quote the poem that is the subject of one of the following essays, the centre cannot hold and mere anarchy is loosed upon the world.

But we cannot live in anarchy; and we always need urgently an answer to the question of how to live. In my opinion, no purely naturalistic answer can answer questions such as What is the good? or What is beauty? or How should we live? The three great quasi-religious movements of our epoch, Marxism, Darwinism and Freudianism, tried to provide 'scientific' answers to these questions, and no doubt the neuroscientism will also soon make its attempt to answer them. But will there ever be a purely scientific procedure to distinguish right from wrong, or ugliness from beauty? Will we ever be able to put a man in some kind of machine and know not only that he is judging and what he is judging, but whether or not his judgment is right? I do not think so; and while this is so (and I suspect will always be so), and while no metaphysically indubitable grounds of judgment will ever be found, it will nevertheless remain necessary for men to make judgments.[1] We shall never be able to put a man in a scan, show him a picture of a tree and conclude any more than that he finds it beautiful. We shall never be able to conclude from his scan that the tree is beautiful; and while some philosophers might argue that nothing is good or beautiful but thinking makes it so, most of us believe as strongly as we believe anything that beauty and goodness are not purely subjective, are not mere constructs of our minds.

Questions of the purpose, if any, of our existence will remain with us always – by always I mean so long as humanity

---

1 By men, of course, I mean women too. It seems to me rather sad that in these days of abject literal-mindedness, one has to point it out.

continues to exist. In the short essays that follow, Ken Francis and I, who come at the world from a different viewpoint, reflect on how authors have answered those questions that cannot be answered and yet must be answered.

Introduction
Kenneth Francis

I LIVE BESIDE THE SEA, which is near an old train station. One beautiful sunny day during summer a few years ago, I was driving towards the railway. The scenery was beautiful, with the ocean, rocks, and a train, like a tiny model locomotive in the far distance, slowly approaching the village.

As I drove near to the station, briefly stopping at the traffic lights, I could see a blind, elderly gentleman with a white stick. He was entering a narrow, arched gateway at the station's entrance. I felt sorry for him and his struggle, as well as his disability preventing him from seeing the wonderful sights on such a glorious day.

However, as he entered the little gateway, another blind man, some ten years younger, was exiting. Both men bumped into each other, as if gently 'fencing' with their white sticks. The scene could have come straight out of a Samuel Beckett play.

When the men departed, the one exiting had a broad smile on his face. Was he 'seeing' the humour in this mini-Theatre-of-the-Absurdesque encounter? All that was missing from the scene, if God does not exist, was the poignant soundtrack of Erik Satie's 'Gymnopedie No.1'. Despite one of the men smiling, if there is no God, then the above incident is no laughing matter.

It's worse than absurd: it's terrifying. In fact, almost all of existence is the stuff of nightmares, if God does not exist and we fully comprehend what Naturalism really is. But believing in God for comfort and hope alone is really no reason to do so. His existence is either true or false. Yet in the 21st century in the remnants of a fragile Christian culture in the West, it seems Existentialism is the new 'religion'. However, such a world view is truly nauseating when all its intellectual ugliness is exposed. And nowhere better is such a world portrayed than in both Theatre of the Absurd dramas and the writings of the great Existentialist philosophers.

As atheist philosopher, Friedrich Nietzsche, declared God dead at the end of the 19th century, nobody is held morally responsible any longer. In the words of a Dostoyevsky character, everything is permitted if God does not exist. And everything is absurd. Don't be deluded by the popular New Atheism that passes for Humanism. This is nothing more than nihilism locked in a cage or piggy-backing on the morals of a struggling, fragile Christianity.

Think about it: in the predominantly Godless Theatre of the Absurd that is the 21st century West, objective moral values and duties could not exist. Love would be an illusion caused by electro-chemical reactions in the brain; charity, a vast vanity, virtue-signalling project or driven by guilt-ridden impulses or personal financial gain.

There would also be no ultimate meaning in an amoral, uncaring universe without purpose. In such a cosmos composed entirely of matter, space and time, the laws of maths and logic would be non-existent because both are immaterial (you can't hit logic or the number 6 with a hammer). Furthermore, rational beliefs on metaphysics would be non-existent because, according to Naturalism, survival of the fittest is devoid of metaphysical belief faculties.

And murder and rape would be neither good nor evil, just culturally inconvenient taboos or acting out of fashion (if a beast in the jungle forcibly copulates with another of his species, surely that's not rape? And if we are no different than animals in a Godless world, isn't such a blind physical act, void of free will, the same? In the same way tigers don't murder, they kill, and hyenas don't steal, they take?).

More: funerals would be events where advanced worms 'mourn' the rearrangement of atoms in wooden boxes, as well as death ending at the grave. In fact, all our earthly endeavours would one day become undone in the heat death of the universe. Think about it: without God, at some point in the future, the lights and heating in the cosmos will be extinguished. The carcasses of dead stars and planets will drift off into the dark, freezing corners of a universe destroyed by decay: the Second Law of Thermodynamics on its last breath.

In summary: without God, we are left with no Absolute Truth, Meaning, Author, History, Writings, Interpretations, Thinker, Laws of Thought, Good, Right or Wrong. We are all alone, rudderless, trying to keep afloat in a Theatre-of-the-Absurd ship of fools. Dostoevsky asks in The Brothers Karamazov: 'How will man be after that [death of God]?' A rational person would say, 'very confused and lost'.

And to quote the ghost of Nietzsche's 'Madman', once we 'wipe away the horizon with a sponge' and 'unchain the Earth from the sun', are not all things in reality subject to subjective psychology, relativistic language and the will to power? And it gets more confusing when we must deconstruct all historical accounts of the past since 'they are relative and not objective'. God becomes redundant, and Jesus of Nazareth becomes whoever we want him to be – a harmless ancient hipster, or worse, a fraud.

To the postmodernist, history is objectively unknowable. The historical relativist will say: 'The event itself, the facts, do not say anything, do not impose any meaning. It is the historian who speaks, who imposes a meaning'. But how can he know that something is not objective history? Does he have an objective knowledge of history that enables him to say that a particular view of history is not objective?

History aside, what about the contemporary world in which we live? Would a relativist fly onboard a plane with a blind sculptor as pilot? And if he had a dry cough, what instructions on a bottle of sulphuric acid or a bottle of Benylin would the postmodern relativist trust to cure his ailment? According to the Critical Theory of Postmodernism, is not the text on such labels relative?

As someone who believes in Logos, I'd favour Benylin over sulphuric acid any day to alleviate my cough. I'd also favour an experienced pilot over a blind sculptor to fly the plane I'm travelling in. Despite seeing the world in a fallen state, it nonetheless makes sense and is intelligible.

But the writings from Ecclesiastes, Existentialism, to Theatre of the Absurd captures brilliantly a Godless universe. Both Dr Dalrymple (who is not religious) and I (a theist) hope to analyse our favourite selections of such great works in a series of essays in the coming chapters, as well as commenting on one play in dialogue from theistic and atheistic perspectives. In this novel approach, it's possible *The Book of Ecclesiastes* got it wrong when it said, 'there is nothing new under the sun'.

CHAPTER ONE

The Book of Ecclesiastes
Theodore Dalrymple

ECCLESIASTES, LIKE ALL OTHER BOOKS IN THE BIBLE, is readable to me only in what used in England (before the Church of England rejected its own liturgy and ran after the false god of modernity) to be called the Authorised Version, but is now universally known as the King James Version. All subsequent translations seem to me to have the verbal felicity of bureaucratic circulars: and if ever a literary work needed or merited poetic felicity, it is Ecclesiastes.

It is a book of wisdom rather than of knowledge, and clearly makes a distinction between the two: knowing how to live and knowing facts about life, or about anything else, are very different, though knowledge about how to live can never be complete, as Ecclesiastes itself warns us. The distinction between knowledge and wisdom is perhaps now more important to appreciate than ever before, in so far as the information age, in which everyone by the touch of a button may find out almost anything that has ever been known (and much else besides), encourages us to think thereby that we may attain knowledge and the wisdom to apply it.

There is perhaps no better corrective to hubris, or Man's temptation to promethean limitlessness (another feature of our age), than Ecclesiastes, as well as a curb to individual pride in personal achievement. For what does it all come to in the end? The very commencement of its disquisition on life tells us: 'Vanity of vanities, all is vanity.'

No one knows precisely when Ecclesiastes was written: the consensus of scholars ('in much study is weariness of the flesh') is that it was composed between 450 and 180 BC. Moreover, one is obliged to use the passive voice about its composition, for no one knows who wrote it, or in what circumstances. It seems to me astonishing, then, that it should have lost none of its salience in the succeeding millennia; on the contrary, it is of greater relevance to our lives, and if I may so put it, to our existential stance towards life, than ever before.

At first sight, Ecclesiastes might seem extremely depressing. Vanity of vanities, all is vanity, the famous assertion with which it opens, is not such a thought as immediately to gladden the heart or encourage effort in one's day to day existence. Much of what follows is in similar vein: for in the midst of activity, to which we ascribe so much importance, we are in vanity. All activity, all effort, ends in the same way, oblivion and forgetfulness: for 'There is no remembrance of former things; neither shall there be any remembrance of things that are to come with those that shall come after.'

This, perhaps, is not strictly or literally true: we do praise famous men, or at least remember them if they do deeds of exceptional evil. But the vast majority of even the most closely-documented life is lost forever, and we still do not know much about the daily life, let alone the inner life, of Shakespeare, though the Folger Library in Washington D.C. has half million books about him. Our childhoods, in which so much was of passionate importance to us, leaves no reliable trace in our mind; and when I look through my own copious notebooks of only a few years ago, I am unable to decipher them, though what I wrote in them must have been of importance to me at the time. For the vast majority of us, then, the words of Ecclesiastes just quoted are literally true. Who can walk through an old cemetery and see all those neglected tombstones sacred to the memory without reflecting on how fleeting that memory is?

Ecclesiastes informs us of the futility of materialism (the avidity to possess, not the philosophical doctrine): 'He that loveth silver shall not be satisfied with silver; nor he that loveth abundance with increase: this also is vanity. When goods increase, they are increased that eat them: and what good is there to the owners thereof, save the beholding of them with their eyes?' The miser pores over his gold, but it does not alter the existential limitations of his life by a nanosecond or by an Angstrom unit.

However, it does not follow from the fact that materialism is futile that a more elevated existence (as we who try to live it like to think it) is not similarly futile. 'I turned myself to behold wisdom, and madness, and folly... Then I saw that wisdom excelleth folly, as far as light excelleth darkness. The wise man's eyes are in his head; but the fool walketh in darkness: and I myself perceived also that one event happeneth to them all. Then I said in my heart, "As it happeneth to the fool, so it happeneth even to me"; and why was I then more wise? Then I said in my heart, that this also is vanity.'

Ecclesiastes is an antidote or corrective to pride, or so I take it to be. Winston Churchill famously said of Clement Attlee that he was a modest little man with much to be modest about (in those days, politicians still had a sense of humour, and did not speak as if they believed they were, or had to be, redeemers of the world). But in reality we all have much to be modest about, 'for I said in mine heart concerning the estate of the sons of men, that God might manifest them, and that they might see that they themselves are beasts. For that which befalleth the sons of men befalleth beasts; even one thing befalleth them: as the one dieth, so dieth the other; yea, they all have one breath; so that a man hath no preeminence over a beast: for all is vanity. All go unto one place; all are of the dust, and all turn to dust again.'

What, then, is left of, or for, human existence, if anything at all? 'Behold that which I have seen: it is good and comely for one to eat and to drink, and so to enjoy all the good of his labour that he taketh under the sun all the days of his life, which God giveth him: for it is his portion.'

One should not expect more of life than life can offer, a singularly unwelcome message at a time of the demand that everyone should be able to determine when and how, and perhaps even if, he dies, as an extension of his natural rights: for personal choice is his highest good. If 'To every thing there is a season, and a time to every purpose under the heaven', the season and the time for modern Man is here and now, as and when he wants it. He has no sense of the ultimate vanity of things, he thinks only that his rights have been violated if his wants are not met with promptitude. There is for him no time to weep, no time to mourn, no time to keep silence; the disappointments of life are not inevitable, they are enemies only to be vanquished – though Ecclesiastes tells us that they never can be.

Some, of course, might find Ecclesiastes dispiriting. It offers no hope of a perfect life on earth, or any end to human suffering. Its stoicism might be criticised as leading to the acceptance of what should not be accepted: 'If thou seest... violent perverting of judgment and justice in a province, marvel not at the matter.' All I can say is that, for myself, the awareness that all is ultimately vanity, albeit that 'Whatsoever thy hand findeth to do, you should do it with thy might', is profoundly consolatory, for it places a bridle on one's passions and is a call to a sense of proportion, without which virtues change to vices and good intentions translate into bad actions.

CHAPTER TWO

Ecclesiastes
'Everything is meaningless', if...
Kenneth Francis

A BOOK ON A BRIEF HISTORY of misery throughout literature and theatre would not be complete without mention of the Book of Ecclesiastes. This Old Testament book, the bleakest book in the Bible, could have been written about life today. Ecclesiastes is addressing idolatry and those who ultimately value the materialism of this world and abandon God. In my relatively brief analyses of Ecclesiastes, a Christ-centric approach will dominate the meaning of this fascinating, yet highly pessimistic text. Let's now look at the core parts of this ancient book.

'Everything is meaningless'... And so begins Ecclesiastes. Written approximately 450 BC, the words of the 'Preacher' (King Solomon?), like the acclaimed Existentialists, shows us what a world looks like if we turn our backs on, or deny, God.

This only have I found; God made mankind upright but men have gone in search of many schemes (7:29).

In such a world, a more fitting title for planet Earth would be 'Cold-hearted Orb That Spins Night and Day'. A world where language is reduced to gibberish and morality reduced to relativism. A world riddled with the decadent temptation of brief, earthly pleasures as opposed to focusing on the ultimate meaning of the eternal God of the Bible. A world where love would be the insignificant, coincidental bumping into each other of two advanced evolved germs, clinging onto a speck of solar muck, orbiting a giant ball of fire lost somewhere in outer space. A world permeated with cruelty, ultimate injustice, frustration, no truth or meaning. In a nutshell, a world where life is freakish and reason is dead.

Ever since Ecclesiastes, numerous paintings, plays, movies and books have likely been inspired, either consciously or unconsciously, by the words of the Preacher. But unlike these latter-day artists' world views, Ecclesiastes, who I believe holds that life has meaning if we give our lives to God, shows us what life is like in an uncaring, amoral, Godless universe.

In such a nightmarish world, we find ourselves in a situation where 'all is vanity' (1:2). This is also summed up quite well in the works of Friedrich Nietzsche and Theatre-of-the-Absurd dramatists, especially in *The Parable of the Madman* and *Waiting for Godot* (which we'll come to later).

Ecclesiastes continues...

> What do people gain from all their labours at which they toil under the sun? Generations come and generations go, but the Earth remains forever. The sun rises and the sun sets, and hurries back to where it rises. The wind blows to the south and turns to the north; round and round it goes, ever returning on its course. All streams flow into the sea, yet the sea is never full. To the place the streams come from, there they return again. All things are wearisome, more than one can say.

Like a Godless universe, the streams are unthinking, uncaring and unaware. The lyrics of 'Ol' Man River'[1] sum this up

---

1 'Ol' Man River' by Jerome Kern, lyrics by Oscar Hammerstein, 1927, from the musical *Show Boat*.

quite well: '*...He [river] just keeps rollin' along... you and me, you know sometimes/We have to sweat, sweat and strain our bodies/ our bodies are all achin'/And wracked with a whole lot of pain... I get weary and so sick of tryin'/I'm tired of livin', and afraid of dyin'...'* The river, just like a Godless universe, doesn't know or care; it just keeps rolling along. But at least there is hope in the song, as it recognises that the Christ knows many earthly things will be forgotten. But not the soul. Ecclesiastes again:

> The eye never has enough of seeing, nor the ear its fill of hearing. What has been will be again, what has been done will be done again; there is nothing new under the sun. Is there anything of which one can say, 'Look! This is something new'? It was here already, long ago; it was here before our time. No one remembers the former generations, and even those yet to come will not be remembered by those who follow them.

In other words, every endeavour, be it good, bad or indifferent, will one day become undone, as death ends at the grave.

> Yet when I surveyed all that my hands had done and what I had toiled to achieve, everything was meaningless, a chasing after the wind; nothing was gained under the sun (2:11)... I devoted myself to study and to explore by wisdom all that is done under the sun. What a heavy burden God has placed on men (1:13).

Unlike the creatures in the animal kingdom, humans are burdened with language and a reflective consciousness. The Romanian philosopher Emil Cioran gives a highly perceptive observation of this: 'A zoologist who observed gorillas in their native habitat was amazed by the uniformity of their life and their vast idleness. Hours and hours without doing anything. Was boredom unknown to them? This is indeed a question raised by a human, a busy ape.

'Far from fleeing monotony, animals crave it, and what they

most dread is to see it end. For it ends, only to be replaced by fear, the cause of all activity. Inaction is divine; yet it is against inaction that man has rebelled. Man alone, in nature, is incapable of enduring monotony, man alone wants something to happen at all costs—something, anything.... Thereby he shows himself unworthy of his ancestor: the need for novelty is the characteristic of an alienated gorilla."[2]

However, Man alienated from God is forever chasing golden calves in his pursuit of his next promiscuous or materialistic fix.

Many animals might not suffer intellectual boredom, but as humans we do. In *Waiting for Godot*, the main characters Vladimir and Estragon wait for someone they are not even sure will turn up. Out of despair, alienation and boredom, they even consider suicide, but are unable to decide who goes first. It's as if Man's spiritual yearnings in this universe can never be satisfied by the physical world. In light of this, Ecclesiastes writes:

> Man's fate is like that of the animals; the same fate awaits them both. As one dies, so dies the other. All have the same breath; man has no advantage over the animal. Everything is meaningless. All go to the same place; all come from the dust and to the dust all return (3:19-20). For with much wisdom comes much sorrow; The more knowledge, the more grief (1:18)... I have seen another evil under the sun, and it weighs heavily on men: God gives a man wealth, possessions and honour, so that he lacks nothing his heart desires, but God does not enable him to enjoy them... This is a grievous evil (6:1-2).

A grievous evil for whom? Those who want instant gratification and become God themselves and do things their way?

A man may have a hundred children and live many years; yet no matter how long he lives, if he cannot enjoy

---

2 Emil Cioran, *De l'inconvénient d'être né* (*The Trouble With Being Born*), Gallimard 1973.

his prosperity…I say that a still born child is better off than he. It comes without meaning, it departs in darkness, and in darkness its name is shrouded. Though it never saw the sun or knew anything, it has more rest than does that man – even if he lives a thousand years twice over but fails to enjoy his prosperity (6:3-6).

Even a stillborn baby is connected to the spirit. The duration of life on this fallen Earth is relatively insignificant compared to the ecstasy of eternity of those saved in the afterlife.

I hated all the things I had toiled for under the sun, because I must leave them to the one who comes after me. And who knows whether he will be a wise man or a fool? Yet he will have control over all the work into which I have poured my effort and skill …So my heart began to despair over all my toilsome labour…for a man may do his work with wisdom, knowledge and skill. And then he must leave all he owns to someone who has not worked for it… What does man get for all his toil and anxious striving – pain and grief: even at night his mind does not rest. This too is meaningless. (2:18-23).

Abandoning God strips one of the ultimate fate of all endeavours and earthly acts.

I have seen something else under the sun: The race doesn't go to the swift or the battle to the strong; nor does food come to the wise or wealth to the brilliant; or favour to the learned; but time and chance happen to them all (9:11)… death is the destiny of every man; and the living should take this to heart. (7:2).

All is in vain: the legacy of the kindness and nurturing of a Mother Teresa is no different to the tyranny and cruelty of a Pol Pot or Joseph Stalin.

There is no remembrance of men of old, and even those who are yet to come will not be remembered by those who follow (1:11). For the wise man, like the fool, will not be long remembered; in days to come, both will be forgotten. (2:16). God has made everything beautiful in its time, and He has set eternity in the hearts of men; yet they cannot fathom what God has done from beginning to end (3:11). As you do not know the path of the wind, or how the body is formed in a mother's womb, so you cannot understand the work of God, the Maker of all things (11:5).

As spiritual beings, we consciously or unconsciously yearn for the transcendence. The secular world of Theatre of the Absurd sucks the awe out of us, leaving us with a feeling of nausea and emptiness. And so wrapped up in our pride, wickedness and restless souls, we feel we can make sense of such a world swirling with molecules in the brains and hearts of hairless apes dressed in suits, skirts, jeans and T-shirts. A world where sex, drugs and mindless Rap are the order of the day: if it feels good, why not 'do it in the road'?[3]

This only have I found; God made mankind upright but men have gone in search of many schemes (7:29).

We reap what we sow.

There is not a righteous man on earth, who does what is right and never sins. (7:20)...one sinner destroys much good. (9:18).

If we don't think promiscuity and sexual deviancy are such a big deal, then it's unlikely we'll repent. The same applies to other worldly vices. The more one tries to live a good, moral life, the more one sees clearly the darkness he once lived in. One day

---

3 'Why Don't We Do It In The Road?' Lennon and McCartney, The Beatles (White Album), 1968.

we will all face ultimate accountability. Finally...

> In the place of justice, wickedness was there (3:16)... I
> thought in my heart, God will bring to judgement both
> the righteous and the wicked (3:17)... Be happy, young
> man, while you are young... Follow the ways of your
> heart and whatever your eyes see, but know that for all
> these things, God will bring you to judgement (11:9).

This summary of Ecclesiastes is just a taste. Volumes have been written on this great book, and hereafter no doubt greater intellects than I will contribute to the discussion of the spiritual consequences of life without God.

The author Douglas Copeland wrote: 'My secret is that I need God - that I am sick and can no longer make it alone. I need God to help me give, because I no longer seem to be capable of giving; to help me be kind, as I no longer seem capable of kindness; to help me love, as I seem beyond being able to love.'[4]

Without God, why should an advanced accidental grown-up germ give, be kind, or love? In the end, none of this proves the existence and necessity of God for humankind, or the spiritual bankruptcy of idolatry. However, we have free will to choose to accept Christ as our Saviour, or else remain trapped in the cold-hearted orb of Theatre of the Absurd. Without Christ, the whole world is chaos. And for the 'blissfully' ignorant, that spiritual chaos dwells deep down in the abyss of the subconscious, disordered soul, thus everything is meaningless.

---

4 Douglas Coupland, *Life After God* (Pocket Books, 1994).

CHAPTER THREE

Swift's *Gulliver's Travels*
Theodore Dalrymple

A MAN'S MEDICAL HISTORY usually explains neither everything nor nothing about him, and Swift's very early
experience of inner ear disease, which ultimately caused him
to go completely deaf, was hardly calculated to cause him to
think well of human existence. Anyone who has suffered even
for a few days what he suffered for much of his life is unlikely to
have thenceforth a completely roseate view of life; and of course
Swift had other reasons for disappointment into the bargain.

But personal bitterness by itself cannot explain Swift's great
masterpiece, for many are the bitter and few are the master-
pieces. Literary genius is capriciously distributed, and therefore
never to be fully explained.

Bitterness of Swift's degree is the consequence of disillu-
sionment that is never quite complete: for if it were complete,
the imperfections of the world would simply be accepted. It is
therefore not resignation or a settled indifference to humanity
that Swift exhibits; it is, rather, a mirror-image of love, a love
that has fermented as it were and gone sour. One might surmise
that Swift despised humanity so much because he would like to
have loved it so much. And, after all, no one criticises anything
with such burning and obviously sincere ferocity as did Swift
criticise humanity without caring deeply about it.

The brilliance of the conception of Lilliput and Brobding-nag is that it allows Swift a conspectus of humanity: he examines it both from afar and from very close up, its absurdly grandiose pretensions and its basic realities. Swift's evident disgust at Man's unavoidable bodily functions, upon whose origins psychoanalysts would no doubt delight to speculate, is surely used metonymically for Swift's far greater disgust at Mankind's moral failings. But again, no one is disgusted by failings unless he believes that better conduct is possible. One might dislike the weather, but not revile or satirise it.

When the King of Brobdingnag says to Gulliver, 'But by what I have gathered from your own relation, and the answers I have with much pains wrung and extorted from you, I cannot but conclude the bulk of your natives to be the most pernicious race of little odious vermin that nature ever suffered to crawl upon the surface of the earth,' he is surely not referring only the race of whom Gulliver is the representative, but of all Mankind, for the sins and deficiencies which he has recounted are of all times and of all places. If they were not, *Gulliver's Travels* – which is about as universal as it is given to literature to be – would not continue to speak so directly to us, but would instead be of interest only to scholars of its age. It is of the nature of great literature to suggest the universal in the depiction of the particular.

Swift's satire on human littleness, absurdity and self-importance is original in form and power, but hardly in sentiment. As Doctor Johnson says (who, incidentally, was a less than whole-hearted admirer of Swift), we need more often to be reminded than informed. We know in our hearts that our importance in the scheme of things is modest. As flies to wanton boys are we to the gods, Shakespeare had already put it through the mouth of one of his characters; and this is so however important we may puff ourselves up individually to be. Gulliver's adventures in Lilliput would remind us, if we kept them in view, that the most powerful and important among us are, fundamentally, no more considerable than the Emperor of Lilliput or Blefuscu and that, if only we were prepared to take a little distance from the disputes on which we were currently engaged, they would appear to us no more sensible than the quarrels of the Lilliputians over the end of the boiled egg by which it should be opened.

The technique of a voyage into an imaginary foreign land allows an author the scope to criticise his own country, culture or religion. The Lilliputians are not absurd in all particulars. Though tiny and ridiculous in others, they have certain laws that hold up a mirror to then-current – and still current – practice:

> They look upon fraud as a greater crime than theft, and therefore seldom fail to punish it with death; for they allege, that care and vigilance, with a very common understanding, may preserve a man's goods from thieves, but honesty has no defence against superior cunning; and, since it is necessary that there should be a perpetual intercourse of buying and selling, and dealing upon credit, where fraud is permitted and connived at, or has no law to punish it, the honest dealer is always undone, and the knave gets the advantage. I remember, when I was once interceding with the emperor for a criminal who had wronged his master of a great sum of money, which he had received by order and ran away with; and happening to tell his majesty, by way of extenuation, that it was only a breach of trust, the emperor thought it monstrous in me to offer as a defence the greatest aggravation of the crime; and truly I had little to say in return, farther than the common answer, that different nations had different customs...

The more things change, evidently, the more they are the same.

One apprehends something similar from Gulliver's visit to Laputa and the Balnibari. Here the people live in a kind of mad defiance of common-sense, neglecting what is before their face and concerning themselves only with the abstruse:

These people are under continual disquietude, never enjoying a minute's peace of mind; and their disturbances proceed from causes which very little affect the rest of mortals. Their apprehensions arise from several changes they dread in the celestial bodies: for instance, that the earth, by the continual approaches of the sun towards it, must, in course of time, be absorbed, or swallowed up; that the face of the sun, will, by degrees, be encrusted with its own effluvia, and give no more light to the world; that the earth very narrowly escaped a brush from the tail of the last comet, which would have infallibly reduced it to ashes; and that the next, which they have calculated for one-and-thirty years hence, will probably destroy us. For if, in its perihelion, it should approach within a certain degree of the sun (as by their calculations they have reason to dread) it will receive a degree of heat ten thousand times more intense than that of red hot glowing iron, and in its absence from the sun, carry a blazing tail ten hundred thousand and fourteen miles long, through which, if the earth should pass at the distance of one hundred thousand miles from the nucleus, or main body of the comet, it must in its passage be set on fire, and reduced to ashes: that the sun, daily spending its rays without any nutriment to supply them, will at last be wholly consumed and annihilated; which must be attended with the destruction of this earth, and of all the planets that receive their light from it.

In the meantime, they live in discomfort in ill-constructed houses; when Gulliver needs a suit of clothes, the tailor measures him by geometric abstractions rather than by the more usual and time-honoured methods, with the result that the clothes are ill-fitting and uncomfortable.

On the island of Balnibari, a college of supposed savants devotes its time to absurd schemes to improve life, for example by extracting sunbeams out of cucumbers, or by ploughing fields with hogs by setting them upon those fields in which acorns have been assiduously buried. Lack of common sense, the chasing of chimeras, leads to impoverishment and degradation, a lesson that is never well-learned. But is on his visit to Glubbdubdrib that Swift's savagery and disgust reach their acme. On that island, necromancers are able to call up the past, and the scales fall from Gulliver's eyes about the moral history of the preceding century:

> Having strictly examined all the persons of greatest name in the courts of princes, for a hundred years past, I found how the world had been misled by prostitute writers, to ascribe the greatest exploits in war, to cowards; the wisest counsel, to fools; sincerity, to flatterers; Roman virtue, to betrayers of their country; piety, to atheists; chastity, to sodomites; truth, to informers: how many innocent and excellent persons had been condemned to death or banishment by the practising of great ministers upon the corruption of judges, and the malice of factions: how many villains had been exalted to the highest places of trust, power, dignity, and profit: how great a share in the motions and events of courts, councils, and senates might be challenged by bawds, whores, pimps, parasites, and buffoons. How low an opinion I had of human wisdom and integrity, when I was truly informed of the springs and motives of great enterprises and revolutions in the world, and of the contemptible accidents to which they owed their success.

This is disgust on an epic scale, indicative of a disappointment on an equally epic scale. But yet we also feel that, the bitterness notwithstanding, there is something of enjoyment in it: as if, in his heart of hearts, Swift would not have wished it otherwise, for the exposure of evil is a transcendent goal that gives meaning to life that might otherwise be lacking. Certainly, *Gulliver's Travels* does not cause us to be downcast, quite the reverse, we read it with a song in our hearts: and those who puzzle over theodicy might find it useful to reflect on this.

CHAPTER FOUR

Poe's 'The Tell-Tale Heart'
'I was never kinder to the old man than during the whole week before I killed him'
Kenneth Francis

ONE OF THE WORST TERRORS of existence is the fear of being murdered or badly tortured. We read endless stories of homicide, both fact and fictional, and the ones that spook us most are those carried out by the psychopath. The Moors Murders in the UK during the 1960s were perhaps the most disturbing story of the slaying of innocent children by a couple of deranged 'lovers' (more like partners in murder), Ian Brady and Myra Hindley, but the story of serial killer Jeffrey Dahmer (1960-1994), is not for the fainthearted. Dahmer was a sex killer who not only murdered his 17 victims, but also dismembered their corpses and cannibalised some of them. Before being killed in prison by a fellow inmate, during an MSNBC interview in 1994, Dahmer claimed that Darwinian unguided evolution, which was taught in school, made him believe humans were insignificant animals. Dahmer thanked his father, who was present during the interview, for sending him scientific material on theism. He said: 'I always believed the lie that evolution is truth, the theory of evolution is truth, that we all just came from the slime, and when we died, you know, that was it, there was nothing - so the whole theory cheapens life. I started reading books that show how evolution is just a complete lie. There's no basis in science to uphold it. And I've since come to believe that the Lord Jesus Christ is the true Creator of the heavens and the earth, that it didn't just happen. I've accepted him as my Lord and Savior, and I believe that I, as well as everyone else will be accountable to him. . . . If a person doesn't think there is a God to be accountable to, then what's the point in trying to modify your behavior to keep it in acceptable ranges?'[1]

In the movie the *Texas Chainsaw Massacre*, the psychopath, Leatherface, wears a mask made of human skin. Carrying a chainsaw, which is turned on, he chases his victims before dismembering and then eating them. But not all serial killers or psychopaths are vicious cavemen/women who carry out their evil deeds in such a ghastly manner. There are others who are 'respectable' guys and gals in suits and skirts living seemingly polite, ordinary lives, but also appearing as gentle folk who share bedsits and other such work spaces with their fellow humans. In Edgar Allan Poe's short story, 'The Tell-Tale Heart', we learn about such a fictitious character. This is perhaps Poe's best-loved and most popular tale. The story was first published in January 1842 in the Boston *Pioneer*. The dramatic monologue begins with a narrator talking about nerves, madness, Heaven and Hell. This protagonist does not fit the psycho-monster profile.

> (Abridged version):
> TRUE! —nervous —very, very dreadfully nervous I had been and am; but why will you say that I am mad? The disease had sharpened my senses —not destroyed —not dulled them. Above all was the sense of hearing acute. I heard all things in the heaven and in the earth. I heard many things in hell. How, then, am I mad? Hearken! and observe how healthily —how calmly I can tell you

---

1 'Remember serial killer Jeffrey Dahmer? Darwinism played a role in his crimes too', *Uncommon Descent* website, June 28, 2012.

the whole story.

What is most disturbing about psychopaths both in reality and the world of fiction, is they don't believe they are mad. From Shakespeare to contemporary crime writers, such characters seem to justify their evil deeds. In 'The Tell-Tale Heart', we see the Bible reference in the opening lines from Philippians 2:10: 'That at the name of Jesus, every knee should bow, of things in heaven, and things in earth, and things under the earth'. There is no doubt that the narrator is a psychopath. And it's difficult to determine the sex of this character. Poe never mentions the sex of the protagonist (but let's assume the male sex). As for the old man: the protagonist could be either a lodger or carer for him, but it's doubtful that he's his son, as he doesn't refer to the old man as 'father' or 'pop' but instead, 'old man'.

> It is impossible to say how first the idea entered my brain; but once conceived, it haunted me day and night. Object there was none. Passion there was none. I loved the old man. He had never wronged me. He had never given me insult. For his gold I had no desire. I think it was his eye! yes, it was this! He had the eye of a vulture —a pale blue eye, with a film over it. Whenever it fell upon me, my blood ran cold; and so by degrees —very gradually —I made up my mind to take the life of the old man, and thus rid myself of the eye forever.

In some cultures, the eye can be seen as evil, and a glance at whom it falls has the ability to cause great harm The *Encyclopaedia Britannica* describes it as: 'Belief in the evil eye is ancient and ubiquitous... and it has persisted throughout the world into modern times. Those most often accused of casting the evil eye include strangers, malformed individuals, childless women, and old women.'

The eye is also theologically important symbolically because it is believed to be associated with evil. This belief dates back to ancient times in mythology, folklore and religion; in India and the countries around the Mediterranean Sea. It can be seen in Jewish, Islamic (Dajjal), Buddhist and Hindu (Kabandha) faiths. The core idea is that those who possess the eye have the power to harm people or their loved ones by just looking at them.

> Now this is the point. You fancy me mad. Madmen know nothing. But you should have seen me. You should have seen how wisely I proceeded —with what caution — with what foresight —with what dissimulation I went to work! I was never kinder to the old man than during the whole week before I killed him. And every night, about midnight, I turned the latch of his door and opened it —oh so gently! And then, when I had made an opening sufficient for my head, I put in a dark lantern, all closed, closed, that no light shone out, and then I thrust in my head. Oh, you would have laughed to see how cunningly I thrust it in! I moved it slowly —very, very slowly, so that I might not disturb the old man's sleep. It took me an hour to place my whole head within the opening so far that I could see him as he lay upon his bed. Ha! would a madman have been so wise as this. And then, when my head was well in the room, I undid the lantern cautiously —oh, so cautiously —cautiously (for the hinges creaked) —I undid it just so much that a single thin ray fell upon the vulture eye. And this I did for seven long nights —every night just at midnight —but I found the eye always closed; and so it was impossible to do the work; for it was not the old man who vexed me, but his Evil Eye.

The narrator says he was 'never kinder to the old man than during the whole week before I killed him'. This is perhaps the most complex and puzzling of psychopathic behaviour: how someone can be so kind yet instantly change into a monster. When people act 'mad' in bad situations, Ecclesiastes (9:3) says: 'This is an evil in all that is done under the sun, that there is one fate for all men; furthermore, the hearts of the sons of men are full of evil and insanity is in their hearts throughout their lives. Afterwards they go to the dead.'

More from the narrator:

> And every morning, when the day broke, I went boldly into the chamber, and spoke courageously to him, calling him by name in a hearty tone, and inquiring how he has passed the night. So you see he would have been a very profound old man, indeed, to suspect that every night, just at twelve, I looked in upon him while he slept. Upon the eighth night I was more than usually cautious in opening the door. A watch's minute hand moves more quickly than did mine. Never before that night had I felt the extent of my own powers —of my sagacity. I could scarcely contain my feelings of triumph. To think that there I was, opening the door, little by little, and he not even to dream of my secret deeds or thoughts. I fairly chuckled at the idea; and perhaps he heard me; for he moved on the bed suddenly, as if startled. Now you may think that I drew back —but no. His room was as black as pitch with the thick darkness, (for the shutters were close fastened, through fear of robbers,) and so I knew that he could not see the opening of the door, and I kept pushing it on steadily, steadily. I had my head in, and was about to open the lantern, when my thumb slipped upon the tin fastening, and the old man sprang up in bed, crying out — 'Who's there?'

This is surely the worst nightmare for any old person living alone: to wake up in the middle of the night after hearing a sound and crying out: 'Who's there?' Sometimes the silence is worse. The narrator says he kept quite still and said nothing. For a whole hour, he did not move a muscle, and in the meantime he did not hear the old man lie down. He was still sitting up in the bed listening. Then, when he had waited a long time, very patiently, without hearing him lie down, he resolved to open a little crevice in the lantern.

> So I opened it —you cannot imagine how stealthily, stealthily —until, at length a simple dim ray, like the thread of the spider, shot from out the crevice and fell full upon the vulture eye.

The Bible tells us: 'He discovereth deep things out of darkness, and bringeth out to light the shadow of death.' (Job 12:22)
'To give light to them that sit in darkness and in the shadow of death, to guide our feet into the way of peace.' (Luke 1:7-9)

> It was open —wide, wide open —and I grew furious as I gazed upon it. I saw it with perfect distinctness —all a dull blue, with a hideous veil over it that chilled the very marrow in my bones…

The narrator sees only what he wants to see. 'How long must I take counsel in my soul and have sorrow in my heart all the day? How long shall my enemy be exalted over me? Consider and answer me, O LORD my God; light up my eyes, lest I sleep the sleep of death.' (Psalm: 13:2-3)

> …And now a new anxiety seized me —the sound would be heard by a neighbour! The old man's hour had come! With a loud yell, I threw open the lantern and leaped into the room. He shrieked once —once only. In an instant I dragged him to the floor, and pulled the heavy bed over him. I then smiled gaily, to find the deed so far done. But, for many minutes, the heart beat on with a muffled sound. This, however, did not vex me; it would not be heard through the wall. At length it ceased. The old man was dead. I removed the bed and examined the corpse. Yes, he was stone, stone dead. I placed my hand upon the heart and held it there many minutes. There was no pulsation. He was stone dead. His eye would trouble me no more.

The narrator then takes precautions to conceal the body. He dismembers the corpse by cutting off the head, arms and legs. He then takes up three planks from the flooring of the chamber, and deposits all the body parts between the scantlings then replaces the boards. But just as he thought he committed the perfect crime, there comes a knocking on the door.

> … I went down to open it with a light heart, —for what had I now to fear? There entered three men, who introduced themselves, with perfect suavity, as officers of the police. A shriek had been heard by a neighbour during the night; suspicion of foul play had been aroused; information had been lodged at the police office, and they (the officers) had been deputed to search the premises. I smiled, —for what had I to fear?

> …They sat, and while I answered cheerily, they chatted of familiar things. But, ere long, I felt myself getting pale and wished them gone. My head ached, and I fancied a ringing in my ears: but still they sat and still chatted. The ringing became more distinct: —It continued and became more distinct: I talked more freely to get rid of the feeling: but it continued and gained definiteness —until, at length, I found that the noise was not within my ears. No doubt I now grew very pale; —but I talked more fluently, and with a heightened voice. Yet the sound increased —and what could I do? It was a low, dull, quick sound —much such a sound as a watch makes when enveloped in cotton. I gasped for breath --and yet the officers heard it not.

Poe's narrator's conscience seems to have got the better of him. It's obvious that the pounding heartbeat he hears so loudly is in his imagination, activated by his disordered soul and descent into paranoia and despair. Although a fictional character, in reality only God can redeem such a man and set him free. Poe, too, had his own troubled soul to cope with, but we'll never know if he made peace with his Maker.

The narrator gets agitated:

> I talked more quickly —more vehemently; but the noise steadily increased. I arose and argued about trifles, in a high key and with violent gesticulations; but the noise steadily increased. Why would they not be gone? I paced the floor to and fro with heavy strides, as if excited to fury by the observations of the men —but the noise steadily increased. Oh God! what could I do? I foamed —I raved —I swore! I swung the chair upon which I had been sitting, and grated it upon the boards, but the noise arose over all and continually increased. It grew louder —louder —louder! And still the men chatted pleasantly, and smiled. Was it possible they heard not? Almighty God! —no, no! They heard! —they suspected! —they knew! —they were making a mockery of my horror! —this I thought, and this I think. But anything was better than this agony! Anything was more tolerable than this derision! I could bear those hypocritical smiles no longer! I felt that I must scream or die! and now —again! —hark! louder! louder! louder! louder!
>
> 'Villains!' I shrieked, 'dissemble no more! I admit the deed! -—tear up the planks! here, here! —It is the beating of his hideous heart!'

Guilt in the world of fiction and beyond has driven many a character insane. We see it in Lady Macbeth, when, in a state of unconsciousness, she sleepwalks and tries to wash the hallucinatory blood off her hands (she manipulated her husband to kill the king). The obsession to repeatedly wash her hands clean indicates her desire to rid herself of the burden of guilt over the murder, of which she unconsciously feels guilty. She commands the blood spot to disappear from her hands: 'Out damned spot! Out I say!' Poe's narrator is in a similar predicament. The loud auditory sound of a heartbeat drives him insane to the point of admitting the evil deed. But like most great literature of crime and punishment, there is a massive paradox: The terror of existence, as well as profoundly affecting these characters' lives and causing great anxiety to many, never fails to amuse us. Imagine the Poe story from a more harmonious angle, entitled, 'A Heart of Gold': A lodger, who lives in a house with an old man, looks after the pensioner's needs and they all live happily ever after. Doesn't have the same appeal, does it?

CHAPTER FIVE

Camus' *L'Étranger*
Theodore Dalrymple

O NE OF THE MANY STRANGE THINGS about Albert Camus' first, and still most widely read, book, *L'Étranger*, is the date of its first publication, 1942. This, of course, was in the middle of a cataclysmic war enveloping practically the whole world, in which Camus himself participated as an active member of the French Resistance (this distinguished him from many other French intellectuals, whose attitude to, or at least conduct during, the Occupation was far more equivocal).

Whatever else may be said about war (if not exactly in its favour, being a calamity to be avoided in most, if not quite in all, circumstances) is that it solves at a stroke (if only temporarily) all questions about the meaning of life. During war, the meaning of life is avoiding death and defeating the enemy. Camus himself had no doubts whatever about the necessity of defeating the Nazis, which suggests that he had at least a negative conception of the meaning of life. Whatever else it meant, life could not mean living under Nazi rule.

In this way, then, 1942 was an odd year in which to publish a book as nihilistic as *L'Étranger*. But even without awareness of the year of its publication, as I was when I first read it, I think I found something in its tone that was insincere or bogus and hence unpleasant. Sincerity in literature may not always be a virtue, but insincerity is almost always a vice.

No one could be as disabused with life as its narrator and protagonist, Meursault, for if one were as disabused as all that, one would hardly bother to commit one's thoughts to paper. Though the book is short, writing even a hundred pages takes considerable effort, as anyone who has tried it will attest. Indeed, to write a book as chiselled in its prose as this takes much effort and self-discipline: verbiage comes much more naturally, as Pascal, who apologised for the length of his letter because he had no time to write a shorter one, knew very well.

Now of course it is a cardinal error to mistake a character's opinions for those of the author. If every character expressed the opinion of the author, there could hardly be disagreement between characters in a book, except in so far as an author could not make up his mind which opinion of his characters was the correct one.

But in the case of *L'Étranger,* there are grounds for supposing that the protagonist is, if not Camus himself, at least someone much resembling him, at least in his philosophical outlook. After all, in his journalistic work published before the book, Camus used a pseudonym almost identical to that of the protagonist of *L'Étranger.* Moreover, the insistence of the lack of objective moral meaning to human existence that the protagonist demonstrates by his actions was precisely that about which Camus was more explicit.

Meursault is (as was Camus himself) a Frenchman born, bred and resident in Algeria, then under French rule, of course. This puts him in a liminal or marginal position: he is not fully French, but he is certainly not Arab either. When, after the world war, the Algerian nationalists began to fight for power (not for freedom), Camus remained ambivalent. He could not support the status quo, but he could not fully support the nationalists either. In the abstract he was right, but the choice was not an abstract one.

The very first line of the book - one of the most memorable in all literature - rang to me somehow inauthentic:

Mother died today. Or maybe yesterday: I can't be sure.

Is anyone really as disabused as this? The natural continuation of these words is 'And good riddance,' for one might have expected someone capable of writing this to have hated his mother. But Meursault gives us no reason to think that he did hate his mother, or that his mother was in any way hateful. In fact we are given no information about her whatsoever; she might as well have been an inanimate object, and an unremarkable one at that, for all that we are told of her.

Meursault goes to the old people's home where his mother resided, and there, while keeping vigil over his mother's coffin, declines to take a last look at her, instead drinking a cup of coffee and smoking a cigarette. His interest appears to be entirely absorbed in the here and now, for example the appearance and conduct of the other old people in the home. Of his own past we hear nothing, as if life consisted of a long series of moments with nothing whatever to connect them.

The protagonist is utterly disconnected affectively from the world as well as his own and his mother's past. His one love affair as described in the book might just as well have been between two lower animals for all its emotional meaning to him. Sex is an itch that has to be scratched, that is all. The sun, the sea and the sand are all that arouse his pleasure. Meursault lives in an eternal present moment, precisely because the past and hence the future mean nothing to him.

The main event of the book is the murder of an Arab on the beach by Meursault for no very adequate reason, on only a trifling pretext. The Arab on the beach, who remains unnamed, has almost no personal characteristics whatever: he is simply an Arab, presumably one of millions. There is no indication that Meursault feels the slightest remorse or even regret at what he has done. The man is dead; he did it; there is nothing more to be said. Even being sentenced to death for his crime does not mean very much to him.

In so far as any explanation is offered for his conduct, it is as follows:

It was the same sun as on the day that I buried Maman and, like then, my forehead especially was hurting me, all of the veins pulsating beneath the skin.

It was hot, so I killed a man, this seems to be the explanation. One is reminded of the answer given to the inmate of Auschwitz who asked why the Nazis were doing this: *Hier ist kein warum*, here there is no why.

If Meursault is not Camus himself, he was certainly no antihero to him either. Indeed, Camus was rather upset when readers saw something despicable in Meursault. He thought they were being philosophically crude or simpleminded, moralistic in the worst way.

I have never read, however, any explanation, at least that I have been able to follow, of the philosophical significance of this book, however brilliant it might be as a literary artefact. A year after its publication, Jean-Paul Sartre, in an essay on the book, wrote:

> *L'Étranger*... plunges us with commentary into the 'climate' of the absurd... Now the absurd is divorce, disconnection. *L'Étranger* is therefore a novel of disconnection, divorce and disorientation...

I confess that this leaves me none the wiser: for disconnection cannot exist without there having first been connection, disorientation is impossible without there having been orientation, and divorce implies divorce from something. I cannot help but think of what Byron wrote at the beginning of Don Juan regarding Coleridge's new-found role:

> Explaining metaphysics to the nation.
> I wish he would explain his explanation.

The absurd, if it means anything at all, must mean the lack of any transcendent purpose in the universe; that all that exists just is, and all that happens just happens. For only a universe that had a design, and hence a designer, could not be absurd in Camus' sense. If Meursault is not an antihero, then, it can only be because everything is permitted since God does not exist. The universe being without meaning, there is no difference between doing good and doing evil.

This no man can believe, at least no man who is not brain-damaged, irrespective of his religious views; he cannot live as if it were true, any more than he can live as if there were no difference between beauty and ugliness. And certainly Camus himself was not such a man. His moral commitments were legion, for example against the death penalty in any circumstances whatever.

When I first read the book, many years ago, I was troubled by the coldness, incuriosity and dehumanising indifference of Meursault towards his victim. I could not then, and still cannot, invest the murder with any philosophical significance beyond the simple and obvious judgment that it is a gratuitous act of evil. Not all the talk of the absurd can disguise, lessen or extenuate that evil. When I read the book for the first time, I did not see how any North African who read it could be other than deeply offended by it, though I had no particular knowledge of or sympathy with North Africans at the time.

Such was Camus' fame and status as a winner of the Nobel Prize at an early age that it took seventy-one years for an Arab view of the book to make itself known in the west. The Algerian writer, Kamel Daoud, wrote *Meursault, contre-enquête*, recounting the story through the eyes of the victim's brother. Of course, this in itself was a tribute to the book's power; but where Camus's book has to me an air of sophisticated insincerity, Daoud's book has that of a burning sincerity.

CHAPTER SIX

Sartre's *Nausea*
A fat worm in a mountain of skulls
Kenneth Francis

I N HIS MOST FAMOUS NOVEL, *Nausea*, the French philosopher Jean-Paul Sartre (1905-1980) wrote about the existential despair of the terror of existence. This book is about a writer who finds himself in the belly of the absurd. Published in 1938, it tells the story of Antoine Roquentin, who returns to France, after many years travelling, to do some research and write a diary.

However, a change has occurred in Roquentin's thoughts and his perception of the world becomes freakish. He feels this change like a strange illness that seems to be progressing; a kind of heightened intellectual vertigo leading to a feeling of nausea. Here Roquentin reflects:

> A little while ago, just as I was coming into my room, I stopped short because I felt in my hand a cold object which held my attention through a sort of personality. I opened my hand, looked: I was simply holding the doorknob. This morning in the library, when the Self Taught Man came to say good morning to me, it took me ten seconds to recognise him. I saw an unknown

face, barely a face. Then there was his hand like a fat worm in my hand. I dropped it almost immediately and the arm fell back flabbily. There are a great number of suspicious noises in the streets, too...[1]

Here we have a deeply confused man with a disordered soul in a world he likely believes is void of God and the moral order. A man who now perceives things similar to how an alien from a different galaxy might see them on arrival to earth. He's metaphorically taken the Matrix 'red pill' and fallen head-first out of Plato's cave.

Everything has become magnified and uncanny, tinged with a feeling of nausea. Few of us are acutely aware of opening a door handle, but, for Roquentin, such a mundane act would have all the trappings of a fat worm-like hand squeezing something cold to gain entrance into another space. If ignorance is bliss, then *Nausea* is hell. A kind of melancholy of all things done without having done all things.

More than likely, *Nausea* was autobiographical. Sartre was a hardboiled atheist and, despite being a popular philosopher, his vision of a Godless world was highly perceptive, but ultimately flawed. If he believed Man is fully responsible for his nature and choices, then why stop at Man? Why not reprimand our garden lawns for overgrowing during the summer months? Or imprison a cat for 'murdering' a mouse?

In the Monty Python sketch 'Mrs Premise and Mrs Conclusion', the former tells her friend she just spent four hours burying her cat alive in order to go on holiday. They then decide to ring Jean-Paul Sartre. When 'Mrs Sartre' answers the phone, Mrs Premise asks is he free, to which she's told, 'he's spent the last sixty years trying to work that one out'.[2]

As for Roquentin's crisis and search for freedom from insanity, that is tragic, albeit the struggle of a fictitious character. His predicament is a kind of solipsism, where his conscious-

---

1 Jean-Paul Sartre, *Nausea*, 1938 (New York: Directions, 1964), p. 11.

2 *Monty Python's Flying Circus*, 'Mrs Premise and Mrs Conclusion', Season Three, Episode One, Whicker's World, 1973.

ness interacts with images in a hyper-aware state. In this hell, there are not only other people, but a perceiver struggling to normalise 'reality'.

Here, the perceiver is not so much struggling to find out whether other minds exist, but is striving to connect and engage with them to avoid subjugation and the decent into madness. According to Sartre: 'To study the way in which my body appears to the Other or the way in which the Other's body appears to me amounts to the same thing... The structures of my being-for-the-Other are identical to those of the Other's being-for-me'.[3]

What Sartre means here, is, since he is his body, he arrives at bodily self-consciousness only when he has the concept of his body as it is for others. Unlike the madman in Poe's 'Tell-Tale Heart'[4] whose acute disease had sharpened his senses, not destroyed them, Roquentin's decent into the maelstrom of despair worsens. He enters a public park which leads onto a beach.

> Never, until these last few days, had I understood the meaning of 'existence'. I was like the others, like the ones walking along the seashore, all dressed in their spring finery. I said, like them, 'The ocean is green; that white speck up there is a seagull,' but I didn't feel that it existed or that the seagull was an 'existing seagull'; usually existence hides itself. It is there, around us, in us, it is us, you can't say two words without mentioning it, but you can never touch it. When I believed I was thinking about it, I must believe I was thinking of nothing, my head was empty, or there was just one word in my head, the word 'to be'.

For Roquentin, the sea belonged to the class of green slimy objects, its colour a quality of the ocean. Living in the now, things look like collapsed scenery to him. Raw existence had unveiled itself to him. For those afflicted with the terror of ex-

---

3 Sartre, *Being and Nothingness* (1943), p. 339.

4 Edgar Allen Poe, *Tell-Tale Heart*, The Pioneer (1843).

istence as experienced by Roquentin, our worldly order and everyday objects disappear into the abyss of the grotesque.

Torn away from the phenomenological beautiful scenery of reality, the sea becomes an enormous swamp, beneath which, high mountains and dark valleys filled with hideous creatures devour each other every second of every hour of every day. Roquentin might be free and experience 'being', but the burden of responsibility of existential freedom is overwhelming.

This psychological-philosophical dilemma is the result of faulty thinking and a Godless worldview. A theatre of the absurd is exactly that: absurd. That's not to say some theists in their darkest periods of doubt don't experience curious, nausea moments. The human condition, being what it is, is vulnerable to all sorts of spiritual moments of philosophical reflection. But where there's a way out for the theist, and not just based on wishful thinking or blind faith, the only exit for the existentialist is to 'create' one's world or, in blind despair, commit the fatal unthinkable.

If the amoral universe really is just a brute fact, which is scientifically and theistically absurd, then Roquentin's worldview is unliveable unless he gets 'creative'. In such a Godless world, streets and houses become geometric blocks and plains with cement-shaped objects of all shapes and sizes. The sound of Mozart's 'Requiem' would be nothing more than the primate jungle auditory observations of an ape: vibrations in the air hitting the outer ear then middle ear, transduced into nerve impulses, then... well, the rest are vibrations, molecules and sound-wave frequency. It's nothing more than a noisy racket that the atoms in a brain obey due to the fixed laws of chemistry.

Even the literature and information we read every day would be no more than billions of black, meaningless squiggles on components derived from felled trees and computer software, and not in the sense of an English-speaking person reading Chinese visa versa; but in the sense of a spider walking across a page of Hamlet, experiencing the physical imagery but not its meaning. Is there no exit from this nightmare? Sartre believes there is.

He is against what he calls 'bad faith' and instead encourages being 'authentic'. And although Roquentin is a harmlessly 'authentic' character in a work of fiction, there's a long list of factual infamous despots and psychos influenced by existentialism who exercised their authenticity with gusto. One of those 'authentic' tyrants was Pol Pot. Many years before the Year Zero slaughter of millions began in the mid-1970s in Cambodia, a well-mannered, polite Mr Pot left Cambodia and went to Paris to study radio technology. While there, he was deeply influenced by Sartre and Marxism. According to historian Paul Johnson, it was Sartre's ideas that had inspired Pot's murderous foot soldiers, the Khmer Rouge.[5] When Pot returned to the old country, the only worms that became fat were those feasting on the mountain of skulls he created during his reign of terror.

The Marxist regime, between 1975 and 1979, was responsible for the deaths of an estimated 1.7 million Cambodians through execution, disease or starvation. A nauseating event beyond belief of some of the worst atrocities ever committed on innocent people.

In testimony before a genocide tribunal in Cambodia, Pol Pot's chief jailer, Kaing Guek Eav, said that children were executed to prevent them seeking revenge. In order to save bullets, executioners would hold the children by their legs or feet and smash their heads against tree trunks in the 'killing fields' on the edge of Phnom Penh.

He admitted, 'I am criminally responsible for killing babies, young children and teenagers', referring to photographs he was shown of how the children were killed. 'The horrendous images of the babies being smashed against the trees . . . I didn't recognise it at first. But after seeing the photographs I recalled that it had happened. It was done by my subordinates. I do not blame them because this was under my responsibility.'[6]

This is what happens when human freedom consists in the

---

5 Paul Johnson, 'The Heartless Lovers of Humankind', *The Wall Street Journal* (January 5, 1987).

6 *Irish Independent*, June 9, 2009, 'Pol Pot's chief jailer "smashed up babies"', story by Andrew Buncombe.

ability of consciousness to transcend its material situation and that monster's like Mr Pot and his henchmen are only free if their basic needs as practical organisms are met. Roquentin might not be a Mr Pot and came to accept his 'freedom' in this life, but he's only a fictional character. Mr Pot, whose morally autonomous existentialism was a great comfort to him, was real. It was reported that Pol Pot died in his bed while resting.[7] If there is no God, then there is no ultimate justice. But if there is a God and Pot didn't genuinely beg Christ for forgiveness on his death bed, then Year Zero for him began at the gates of Hell... for eternity.

---

7 David P. Chandler, *Brother Number One: A Political Biography of Pol Pot,* Westview Press, Boulder, CO., (1999, p.186).

CHAPTER SEVEN

Chekhov's 'A Dreary Story'
Theodore Dalrymple

ANTON CHEKHOV WAS TWENTY-NINE years old when he wrote this story, seven years after Tolstoy's *The Death of Ivan Ilyich*, to which some critics have seen as a riposte. Unlike the latter, it provides no glimmer of hope, though one must be careful not to ascribe its despair to its author. It is, after all, a work of fiction, and a character's outlook cannot be taken as the author's own, especially an author as possessed of so much insight into the human heart as Chekhov.

The protagonist and narrator of the story is an emeritus professor of medicine, Nikolay Stepanovitch, who interestingly refers to himself in the third person at the very beginning of his narration. This device establishes that he is attempting to view his own life objectively, in the way of a detached observer, rather than as the subject of it, or even as a participant in it. By this means, we are encouraged to suppose that he is being truthful, that the facts are as he states them. He describes himself as he would describe another.

Outwardly, at least, Nikolay Stepanovitch's life has been a great success. He is a professor renowned and revered not only in Russia but in the whole of Europe who, when he dons all his decorations and honours, is called 'the Ikonstand' by students. But he is now dying, and he looks back on his life as an expense of spirit in a waste of shame. (Incidentally, Chekhov, being a doctor, provides an excellent description of the signs and symptoms that will lead to the Professor's demise. He has both glucose and albumen in his urine. He has swelling of his legs. Since he is aged sixty-two, which was considered old age in 1889 when Chekhov wrote the story, it is clear that he suffers from uncontrolled Type II diabetes which has resulted in kidney failure. Depression and withdrawal are common, almost invariable, concomitants of such kidney failure. What proportion of Nikolay Stepanovitch's despair is attributable to his physical condition?)

His marriage, which once was happy, is now a source of torment to him, his wife merely a constant irritation to him. He is annoyed by his daughter's studies at the Conservatoire, which he considers frivolous and insincere. He has a stepdaughter whom he loved deeply but to whom he has little to say once she became enamoured of the theatre, another realm of triviality and insincerity. The students whom he once loved anger him by their slovenly habits, and those who seek his personal help he considers dishonest wasters. His main assistant and possible successor is a dull pedant, while his daughter's fiancé, a man of German origin called Gnekker (on the matter of Germans, Chekhov obviously agrees with Tolstoy), is a pompous, self-satisfied, unattractive, shifty adventurer. But it is not perfectly clear that the fault lies entirely with others: when, for example, his assistant, Pyotr Ignatyevitch, comes to see him while he is on holiday, he tells us:

> In my present state of mind five minutes of him is enough to sicken me as though I had been seeing and hearing him for an eternity. I hate the poor fellow. His soft, smooth voice and bookish language exhaust me, and his stories stupefy me… He cherishes the best of feelings for me, and talks simply in order to give me pleasure, and I repay him by looking at him as though I wanted to hypnotize him, and think 'Go, go, go!…' But he is not amenable to thought-suggestion, and sits on

and on and on….

Pyotr Ignatyevitch is no worse than a well-meaning bore, and after having taunted him, Nikolay Stepanovitch writes:

> I behave badly with Pyotr Ignatyevich, and only when he is going away, and I catch a glimpse of his grey hat behind the garden fence, I want to call out and say, 'Forgive me, my dear fellow!'

Thus the problem is as much with the narrator as with the world, but he is not alone in having an existential crisis. On reviewing his life, he comes to the conclusion that his exclusive dedication to science has resulted in nothing very great or important. He has lacked what he calls 'a general idea,' that is to say an overarching purpose in life, nor can he think of one now.

His stepdaughter, Katya, suffers from the same lack of purpose, and wants guidance from him which he is unable to give. Possessed of a substantial inheritance, she has run away to join a provincial theatre company, has an affair with an actor and a child by him who quickly dies, but then discovers, or appears to discover, that the actors are all scoundrels merely pretending to be artists. She returns home and sets up in a flat of her own. After a time, she finds her drifting life intolerable and asks Nikolay Stepanovitch what she should do. He suggests that she should return to acting, since the theatre had once been her passion. This suggestion provokes on her part one of the most heart-rending confessions known to me:

> 'Nikolay Stepanovitch, this is cruel!' she cries, and suddenly flushes all over. 'You want me to tell the truth aloud? Very well, if… if you like it! 'I have no talent! No talent and… a great deal of vanity! So there!'

There is a terrible truth in this and we feel her piercing pain as if it were our own. Her complaints against her fellow-actors were actually a smokescreen to prevent her and others from perceiving the hopelessness of her choice of career. Alas, she has no other; and her confession makes us wonder how much of our complaint against the world, or against others, is really an unacknowledged awareness of our own deficiencies.

Nikolay Stepanovitch's daughter, Liza, also has a crisis of nerves. He tries to calm her down but finds he has nothing constructive to say to her. Although Chekhov does not tell us so, we suspect that Liza has her crisis of nerves because she does not know what she wants to do in, or with, her life and is far from sure that she wants to spend it with a man like Gnekker. In other words, hers is a general or existential crisis, not a response to a particular event or situation. 'My kind papa! My dear, good papa... I don't know what is the matter with me... I am miserable!'

Although an eminent professor of medicine, a scholar, an experienced man of the world and father who has tried to be good, he can think of nothing to say or do:

> What could I do? I could do nothing. There was some load on the girl's heart; but I did not understand. I knew nothing about it, and only muttered: 'It's nothing, it's nothing; it will pass. Sleep, sleep!'

This is an avowal of impotence in the face of the largest questions of human existence: how to live and what to live for. Nikolay Stepanovitch thinks of writing a prescription for her, but then decides against it. Nowadays, perhaps, he would have had no such hesitation: he would have prescribed. How many people are prescribed antidepressants and anxiolytics because they do not know how to live or what to do with their lives?

In the final scene of the story, Nikolay Stepanovitch, although himself very ill, exhausted and with not long to live, has gone at his wife's behest to Kharkov, to investigate the background of Liza's suitor, Gnekker. Gnekker has told Liza's parents that his father has a house there and a large estate outside, but when Nikolay Stepanovitch tries to investigate, no one has heard of Gnekker or his father. In short, Gnekker is a pure adventurer.

Shortly after his arrival in Kharkov, Nikolay Stepanovitch receives a telegram from his wife:

Gnekker was secretly married to Liza yesterday. Return.

Liza has married Gnekker, we feel, from despair, not from love; one foresees a long period of misery stretching before Liza as a result.

Nikolay Stepanovitch is numb at the news, and dismayed by his own numbness:

I am dismayed, not by what Liza and Gnekker have done, but by the indifference with which I hear of their marriage. They say philosophers and the truly wise are indifferent. It is false: indifference is paralysis of the soul; it is premature death.

He spends a sleepless night:

And now I examine myself. What do I want?

His answer is bleak: he wants more of what has not satisfied him thus far.

I want our wives, our children, our friends, to love in us, not our fame... but to love us as ordinary men. Anything else? I should like to have helpers and successors. Anything else? I should like to wake up in a hundred years' time and to have just a peep out of one eye at what is happening in science. I should have liked to live for another ten years... What further? Why, nothing further. I think and think, and can think of nothing more. And however much I might think, and however far my thoughts might travel, it is clear to me that there is nothing vital, nothing of great importance in my desires. In my passion for science, in my desire to live, in sitting on this strange bed, and in this striving to know myself – in all the thoughts, feelings and ideas I form about everything, there is no common bond to connect it all into one idea… in all the pictures my imagination draws, even the most skilful analyst could not find what is called a general idea. Or the god of a living man.

And he adds, in a line by itself:

And if there is not that, then there is nothing.

Meanwhile, Katya has managed to trace her stepfather to Kharkov and has followed him there. She arrives at his hotel bedroom.

'Nikolay Stepanovitch,' she says, turning pale and pressing her hand to her bosom – 'Nikolay Stepanovitch, I cannot go on living like this! I cannot! For God's sake, tell me quickly, this minute, what I am to do! Tell me, what am I to do?'

Nikolay Stepanovitch can think of nothing and suggests lunch instead. Katya turns cold, gets up to go, and walks down the hotel corridor without turning back to look at him. We know, and he knows, that he will never see her again.

I've seen her black dress for the last time: her steps have died away. Farewell, my treasure!

A Dreary Story is that of a man with no sense of transcendence who yet needs it. What is the solution to his predicament? Chekhov (unlike Tolstoy) suggest none. Perhaps it does not exist.

CHAPTER EIGHT

Beckett's *Waiting for Godot*
The absurdity of life without God
Kenneth Francis

T HERE IS SOMETHING of 'The Emperor's New Clothes' about Theatre-of-the-Absurd. That's not to say an un-dressed body can't be amusing, if not vaguely intriguing; especially one thrown naked onto a speck of solar dust called Planet Earth, orbiting a giant ball of fire lost in a Godless cosmos.

To the drama critics of yesteryear, the Theatre of the Absurd was always seen as very French. But now in the early 21st century, the denizens of the theatre world are invariably Godless: modern-day 'French', if you will. But there's a difference: The most rebellious, authentic, anti-Establishment thing a 21st century playwright can do, is write a beautiful drama devoid of bleak, ugly, Godless content.

However, back in the day, when those hostile to Christians were anti-Establishment, one such revolutionary play with bleak, ugly, cruel, bizarre, depressing, hopeless, meaningless content was Samuel Beckett's *Waiting For Godot*, which was premiered many years ago at Theatre de Babylone, Paris, in 1953.

In Dublin, Ireland, The Gate Theatre is renowned for producing the best performances of Beckett's plays, especially

'Godot'. When 'Godot' made its way to Dublin some years after its Paris premier, audiences where divided but it soon became popular. This success later resulted in 1991 when the Gate became the first theatre in the world to stage 19 Beckett plays.

I'm a reluctant admirer of Beckett's 'Godot', more fascinated by the Existential theme of his work than its form, which also intrigues me to a lesser degree. I'd rate the plays of Eugene Ionesco superior to Beckett's, but that's just a matter of opinion.

In recent years, it has become hip to like Beckett and I believe, in some ways, genuine admirers of 'Godot' believe it has suffered as a consequence of this due to its popularisation into the mainstream. There seems to be a certain kind of dilettantism, pretentiousness, amongst many of Beckett's fans, due to his plays' dark and interesting content.

That aside, however, in the Gate Theatre's versions of 'Godot' in recent times, the two hapless tramps were usually played by actors Barry McGovern (Vladimir) and Johnny Murphy (Estragon). The pair deliver Beckett's pithy, rambling dialogue to perfection. Barry McGovern is a highly acclaimed versatile freelance actor. He is also the world's leading Beckett actor. I asked him if he thought Beckett was inspired in any way by the *Book of Ecclesiastes* or if 'Godot' has become more relevant today than it was over 60 years ago.

He said:

I think Waiting for Godot and the other plays have stood the test of time because they say more about the experience of what it is to *be* - especially at this time - than any other. I'm not sure that *Ecclesiastes* inspired Beckett. Or that it contains much hope. After all, the main thrust of the book is 'Vanity of vanities... all is vanity'.

Though perhaps the most Beckettian verses are 'Two are better than one, for they have a good reward for their toil. For if they fall, the one will lift up his fellow: but woe to him that is alone when he falleth; for he hath not another to help him up'. *All that Fall* is based on the verse in psalm 145: 'The Lord upholdeth all that fall and raiseth up all those that be bowed down'.

I do think *Waiting for Godot* has some hope. Vladimir quotes (or rather misquotes) Proverbs when he says, 'Hope deferred maketh the something sick' - the something being the heart. And despite all the seemingly futile waiting and disappointment, each act ends, after a resolve to go, with *They do not move.*

They might not move far from the main scene, but the pair constantly complain, argue, play ridiculous games, philosophise and even contemplate suicide. They basically try to kill time while standing around a dead tree on a low mound surrounded by a barren landscape. The barren tree has echoes of Matthew 21:18-22 and Mark 11:12-14. Here we have an account of Jesus cursing a dead fig tree.

Symbolically, this tree stood for the spiritual bankruptcy of ancient Israel, where religiously many, not all, appeared upright outwardly, while inwardly hypocrisy and sinfulness lurked slyly in the depths of their hearts. This, of course, was and still is universal amongst all tribes and groups.

At the centre stage of 'Godot', is such a symbol silently screaming of spiritual death shortly after World War II? Had the play been written today, their constant moaning would probably be punctuated by sporadic glances into their spiritually dead iPhones in search of a Tweet from Godot, with him tweeting back: 'CU2 L8'r'.

Other characters in the play that they meet are Pozzo (a cruel master during first appearance), Lucky (his slave during first appearance) and a boy (a messenger). What is tedious about this tragicomedy is its repetition; what's intriguing about it is its absurdness; and what's tragic about it is the absence of God, meaning, and a seemingly hopeless situation. Beckett once said that Godot did not represent God. However, did he unconsciously mean 'Godot' to be God when he wrote the play, perhaps in a state of trance?

Although he grew up in a Protestant background, the adult Beckett's worldview was certainly atheistic.[1] As for his inspiration for 'Godot', it could lie anywhere from Shakespeare's *King Lear*, Caspar Friedrich's painting 'Two Men Contemplating the Moon', to de Balzac's play *Mercadet*, in which the protagonist waits in vain for an unseen person called Godeau; or Victor Frankl's *Trotzdem Ja Zum Leben Sagen: Ein Psychologe erlebt das Konzentrationslager*; in English: *Man's Search For Meaning*.

However, in Beckett's 'Godot', there are lots of allusions to the Bible in the characters' theological discussions, as well as their physical sufferings and uncomfortable, badly fitted clothes. Vladimir's mention of only one Gospel referring to the thief on the cross being saved is delivered by one who seems to have some knowledge of the Bible but little understanding.

Vladimir: '... how is it that of the four evangelists, only one speaks of a thief being saved. The four of them were there – or thereabouts – and only one speaks of a thief being saved... Come on, Gogo, return the ball, can't you, once in a way?'

The debunking-Christianity remarks of Vladimir (or Beckett) fails to acknowledge that unanimous corroboration in evidence, even in a court of law, can often point to conspiracy to achieve a consensus, favourable outcome, even propaganda. But rigid Gospel analyses, biblical inerrancy and interpretation are for another essay.

It doesn't take away from the fact that this nightmarish situation also has echoes of Sartre's play *No Exit*: an intellectual Hell of eternal suffering, and not that traditionally depicted metaphorically in Christianity or the paintings of Hieronymous Bosch.

'Godot' is certainly not a play about two scruffy men waiting for someone who doesn't turn up. No, Beckett's 'Godot' has such a profound effect in the world of theatre because it touches on one of the greatest scourges of Mankind: boredom and meaninglessness in a Godless universe.

To illustrate a brief antidote to the boredom aspect of the play, imagine the contrast of a pub instead of a barren tree as the

---

1 Francis Doherty, *Samuel Beckett*, London: Hutchinson & Co Ltd., 1971.

centrepiece on the stage of 'Godot'. In such an establishment, our two scruffy heroes would descend into a drunken stupor oblivious to the tedious waiting game for a person who never arrives. That would temporarily sort out the boredom. But the hangover would be horrendous, as the boredom returns and the quest for salvation, meaning and the arrival of Godot would remain elusive if not non-existent.

However, if Beckett was an atheist, it seems, like many atheists, he might have suffered from 'phantom God' or intuitively believed in Him. For the atheist to fully accept (in Naturalism, could 'acceptance' exist?) that he or she is entirely *determined*, life would be intolerable and unlivable.

It's also possible Beckett believed in a deistic God, one who doesn't care for humanity and is distant from the cast of 'Godot' in such a decaying setting. And his characters Vladimir and Estragon mirror such a view. The symbolism in 'Godot' points to the pathos of Man and his wretchedness: both tramps are filthy and Pozzo is initially cruel to Lucky, whom he temporarily controls with a rope. Pozzo and Lucky's first appearance might also point to the determinism a puppet master (Naturalism) has in controlling his (molecular) puppet.

According to Naturalism, we would be unaware molecular puppets going through our earthly motions, thus possibly 'lucky' in our state of cosmic, blissful ignorance. In such a world, Pozzo couldn't be accused of cruelty: how could he ever improve his morality? And the complaining protagonists couldn't complain about the problem of suffering, as any meaningful conversations would be paradoxically meaningless and without moral justification.

The wickedness of Beckett's world is beyond righteous indignation because the world just is and not what it ought to be. Bertrand Russell once wrote that we must build our lives upon the firm foundations of unyielding despair.[2] And what is the despair in 'Godot', if there is any? Is it because the players' lives are out of harmony in a Godless world?

---

2 Bertrand Russell, 'A Free Man's Worship,' in *Why I Am Not a Christian*, ed. P. Edwards (New York: Simon & Schuster, 1957), 107.

The playwright Eugene Ionesco sums up the meaning of despair of the Theatre of the Absurd when he wrote that absurd is that which is devoid of purpose; 'cut off from his religious, metaphysical, and transcendental roots, Man is lost; all his actions become senseless, absurd, useless'.[3]

I can't get inside Beckett's mind or know his motives; I can only speculate on what I think is more probable than improbable. If he was rejecting Logos and embracing avant-garde in turning his back on classical conventions for nihilistic reasons, then I believe he unwittingly gets caught in his own secular net. Why? Such a weird world proves that our existence points to the existence of God by showing us the absurdity of life on Naturalism.

But if, like Brecht, for political reasons, Beckett's play is a deliberate attempt to subvert the effect of catharsis, then it would appear such an anti-Christian narrative showcasing the absence of a cathartic resolution of emotions could possibly sink below consciousness and influence rebellious-type audiences to embrace secularism.

As Secular Man is driven by endless, unachievable desires and with no higher destiny, we can also see Beckett's bleak vision in philosophical literature, music, Surrealist art and cinema: from the Godless Schopenhauer,[4] Wagner,[5] Nietzsche,[6] to Ernst[7] and Bunuel.[8]

No doubt, the expectations of those who saw 'Godot' for the first time were contradicted by the anomalies in the absurd narrative and denouement. This is what happens when the moral order is suppressed or turned upside-down. Whatever the case, my criticism of Beckett's atheistic absurd drama in no

---

3 Eugene Ionesco, *Dans les armes de la ville*, Cahiers de la Compagnie Madeleine Renaud-Jean-Louis Barrault, Paris, No. 20, October 1957.

4 Arthur Schopenhauer, *The World as Will and Representation.*

5 Wagner, *Tristan und Isolde.*

6 Nietzsche, 'Parable of the Madman'.

7 Max Ernst, *At the First Clear Word* (1923).

8 Luis Bunuel, *Cet Obscur Objet du Desir* (1977) and *Le Charme discret de la bourgeoise* (1972).

way proves Christianity to be true, in the same way one cannot prove with ultimate certainty the existence of the external world or other minds other than one's own. But it does prove that existence in such an absurd world is not only irrational, but terrifyingly unliveable.

I believe the most profound sentence in the history of mankind is the opening line in the Gospel of St John (1:1): 'In the beginning was the word'. The Word is Logos: Logic, Language, Truth, Reason, Beauty, Meaning, Moral Order. Ultimately, the Logos is God. And ultimately, 'Godot' is devoid of this. But even the concept of a meaningless universe in ruins is nakedly intriguing, as it paradoxically repels but is also fascinating in its unresolved bleakness.

CHAPTER NINE

Waiting for Godot
Theodore Dalrymple

THE AMERICAN LITTERATEUR, Logan Pearsall Smith, wrote that he once knew a man who was so downcast by the mundane prospect of having to put on his shoes and tie his shoelaces every day that he committed suicide. Estragon's boots in *Waiting for Godot* likewise exhaust him: at the very beginning of the play we see him falling back exhausted as he tries unsuccessfully to remove a boot. This utterly banal act saps his will. 'Nothing to be done,' he says.

There is nothing to be done because nothing can be done: whatever effort you make, everything will, in the deepest sense, remain the same. Your life – everyone's life – is but a period of vacuous consciousness between two eternities of oblivion. We use various feeble expedients to disguise this fact from ourselves, but the more honest we are the more evident and inescapable becomes this fundamental truth about human existence. According to this philosophy, Estragon and Vladimir are exceptionally clear-sighted men.

At the same time, their waiting for Godot is a protest against the meaninglessness of their existence, or of existence itself, and even an expression of the faint but illusory hope that some transcendent meaning might be given to it by a superior being. Although it is always dangerous to argue from a work of imaginative literature to an author's own views, *Waiting for Godot* seems to me to be the work of a man who can see all the advantages and consolations of faith in a personal God, and who in fact was brought up in such a faith, but who cannot assent to it intellectually. Beckett establishes very early on in the play that he is arguing with a religious standpoint that he no longer shares when he quotes (or rather when Vladimir attempts and fails to quote fully, as a dim recollection) the Bible. On the second page of the Faber edition, we read:

ESTRAGON: What do you expect, you always wait until the last moment.

VLADIMIR: [Musingly.] The last moment... [He meditates.] Hope deferred maketh the something sick, who said that?

This, of course, is a quotation from Proverbs, not coincidentally in the version with which he grew up, the King James (or, as he would have known it, the Authorised) version: 'Hope deferred maketh the heart sick: but when desire cometh it is a tree of life.' Again, it is not a coincidence that the very words that Vladimir forgets are 'the heart,' for it is a heartless universe that Vladimir and Estragon inhabit, and Beckett makes the point in a way in which only someone familiar with the Bible would have thought of, and in which few people would make it now. Religion was very much a live presence or question in his mind, even if he rejected it, as it would be for very few secularists of 42 (the age at which Beckett wrote the play) in the present day.

Of course, *Waiting for Godot* is more than a meditation on a Godless world, or an extended argument against a teleological universe. If it were only that it is unlikely that it would have held its place in the repertoire. Very few plays give to the language a phrase that everyone knows and understands, or thinks he understands, irrespective of whether he has ever seen or read the play. When one waits for Godot, one waits for someone, or something, who or that is never going to arrive. This is a universal, or at least a frequent, human predicament, from which I doubt many people in our society could claim to be totally immune. It is the consequence of Man's natural propensity to imagine that somewhere, somehow, there is a perfect sublunary mode of existence, and that some agent or process, currently waiting in the wings, will bring it about. For Marxists it is the classless society in which politics will disappear, government will be the mere administration of things rather than rule over men, and individuals will be exactly what they want to be: brain surgeons in the morning, racing-car drivers in the afternoon, operatic tenors or sopranos in the evening:

> In communist society, where nobody has one exclusive sphere of activity but each can become accomplished in any branch he wishes, society regulates the general production and thus makes it possible for me to do one thing today and another tomorrow, to hunt in the morning, fish in the afternoon, rear cattle in the evening, criticise after dinner, just as I have a mind, without ever becoming a hunter, fisherman, herdsman or critic.[1]

That anyone past the age of adolescence could have given a moment's assent to this drivel, or to the persons capable of producing it, is a tribute to human credulity. Compared with it, the most extravagant of religious notions are extremely hard-headed.

For the purchasers of lottery tickets, Godot is the winning ticket: and if the chance of ever having such a ticket is not quite zero, it approaches zero. Moreover, empirical evidence suggests that sudden access to great wealth, especially when unearned, does not lead to the anticipated felicity: so not only are the chances of winning vanishingly small, but the probability that winning will solve all problems is also tiny.

This is because so few people have any real idea of a better life than the one they are leading. When I asked my patients who said that they wished they were very rich what they would

---

1 Marx and Engels, *The German Ideology.*

then do with their time and money in order to be happy and fulfilled, it was clear they had given no consideration to the matter and could think of nothing more than to live as they were currently living, but at a much higher level of consumption. The hollowness of it was clear to them.

Where religious belief no longer provides any sense of the transcendent or purpose in life, men have to create it for themselves, at least once survival has been assured, as it mostly has: for without the transcendent, suffering (which can only be postponed, not avoided altogether) has no meaning and is therefore all the worse. Vladimir and Estragon are waiting for Godot to fill the void: by the end of the play (and really from the beginning) we know that he will never show up, that the void will never be filled.

Where the transcendent does not come from belief in God, it must be this-worldly. One such purpose, popular in the modern world, is the achievement of power on whatever scale satisfies us – though there is an inherent tendency for the lust for power to grow, and a sufficiency of power a mirage that recedes as you approach it.

The story of Pozzo and Lucky (if it can be called a story) illustrates the vanity of power in a symbolically compressed way. In the first act Pozzo gives orders to Lucky in an entirely arbitrary and indeed cruel way; his power seems to be exerted for no purpose beyond its own exercise; he does not explain himself to Lucky, even ordering him to think without giving any indication as to what he should think about. It suggests that, without orders, Lucky's mind is blank, he is an automaton.

In the second act, however, which is set only a day later, Pozzo is blind and stumbling. He has gone overnight (without any explanation as to how or why, except the march of time) from being prepotent to pathetic. This is the inevitable fate of the self-important; against time and decay there is no defence, and power comes to look merely ridiculous. Look on me, o ye mighty, and despair!

The vanity of ambition or any other human goal could have been illustrated in a very similar way. Literary immortality, for example, is not only uncertain, but lasts a footlingly short time by comparison with the age of the universe. But most people – certainly not Vladimir and Estragon – do not aspire even to such limited supposedly transcendent goals. When they try to remember what they did yesterday, they conclude that they must have blathered the day away, not because they actually remember having done so, but because (so they say) that is what they have done for the past fifty years. Furthermore, their talk is blather not because of any deficiency on their part, but because all talk like all action is futile: there is no possibility of it being otherwise.

Thus purposelessness pervades everything: nothing is significant because nothing could be significant. 'Nothing happens, nobody comes, nobody goes, it's awful.'

In the circumstances all human activity is but diversion from the emptiness of existence. When Pozzo and Lucky exit in the first act, Vladimir says (after a long pause that suggests vacancy), 'That passed the time' as if time were something to be endured. Estragon replies, 'It would have passed in any case.' In other words we can neither speed nor slow it, and have no control over the entire medium in which we live our lives. Which of us, by taking thought, can add one cubit to his stature?

Human aspiration is ridiculous and destined to be thwarted. But even aspiration, in the last analysis, is impossible. Discussing that they would ask of Godot were he, *per impossibile*, to arrive, Vladimir says, 'Oh… nothing very definite.'

ESTRAGON: A type of prayer.
VLADIMIR: Precisely.
ESTRAGON: A vague supplication.
VLADIMIR: Exactly.

They don't even know, then, what they aspire to.

Although Beckett denied more than once that Godot was God, his denial is not credible, at least to me. The following dialogue brings the 'Second Coming' irresistibly to mind:

ESTRAGON: He should be here.
VLADIMIR: He didn't say for sure he'd come.
ESTRAGON: And if he doesn't come?
VLADIMIR: We'll come back tomorrow.
ESTRAGON: And then the day after tomorrow.
VLADIMIR: Possibly.
ESTRAGON: And so on.

Hope and expectation are alike illusions.

The strange thing is, of course, that Beckett did not live as if this were true. In his youth he was a fine athlete and even played first-class cricket (a little), which he most certainly could not have done unless he took the game seriously and practised hard to get better at it, suggesting that he saw it as a worthwhile goal. In the Second World War, during the Occupation, he risked his life in the Resistance, suggesting that personally he was no moral nihilist. He was very particular about how his plays should be produced and performed, which suggests that he did not think them entirely insignificant. Finally, his disposition, character and personality were not at all what one might have supposed of the author of such a play.

Does this imply, then, that his play refers only to the inability of most people to find meaning and purpose in life without God, and that there are certain people – playwrights, for example – who can do happily without Him? Is the inability to find meaning and purpose an existential one or a sociological one? The text says one thing and the author's life another – as is often the way.

CHAPTER TEN

Q&A on *Waiting For Godot*
Kenneth Francis and Theodore Dalrymple

KF: You say: 'Godot seems to me to be the work of a man who can see all the advantages and consolations of faith in a personal God, and who in fact was brought up in such a faith, but who cannot assent to it intellectually.' But there are also great advantages in the moral autonomy of atheism, *if true*, as well as the consolation that Hell does not exist. Perhaps Beckett's faith was blind faith, as opposed to faith based on deep intellectual reasoning. It's difficult to understand how disbelief in God is intellectual, when according to Naturalism, the probability of having reliable cognitive faculties for metaphysical truths is extremely low, if not zero. As Charles Darwin rightly acknowledged: 'Would any one trust in the convictions of a monkey's mind, if there are any convictions in such a mind?'[1] The Christianity preached in 20th century Ireland (both Catholic and Protestant) was and still is in many ways anti-intellectual. And that's probably why Beckett didn't seem to have a grasp of sophisticated theology. He confers freedom of the will on his main characters in Godot, which contradicts his Godless message. Also, surely in a meaningless world, communicating such struggles on stage would be without meaning and thus a waste

---

1 Darwin Correspondence Project, letter, Darwin, C.R. to Graham Williams, July 3, 1881.

of time. Beckett had a reputation for being kind to others, as well as generous with his money. However, his bleak, despairing vision offers no hope for humanity. It seems Beckett wants to have his theatrical cake and eat it too, by being intrigued by certain theological/philosophical ideas without believing in them. Most contemporary theist philosophers also don't believe in the straw-man caricature god that Beckett or even the New Atheists disbelieve in. In light of this, don't you think Beckett's theological views lack sophistication, despite him paradoxically touching impressively on many important elements of a Godless world?

TD: I agree with you that Beckett seems to want to have his cake and eat it by proclaiming meaningfully that everything is meaningless. In his view, though (or perhaps I should say the view that seems to be propagated in the play) it is not a waste to time to proclaim the meaninglessness of everything because, everything being meaningless, there is no proper use to which time could be put and therefore no possibility of wasting it. How we fill our time is thus a matter of complete moral indifference; and if we choose to spend it on puzzling over plays such as 'Godot', it is as good as – though not better than - spending it on polishing our shoes or reading Agatha Christie. We ought to remember (personally I keep forgetting) that we are discussing a literary work and not a philosophical treatise. We assume that Beckett would have assented himself to whatever philosophy is the philosophy that 'Godot' yields when correctly interpreted. Perhaps he was merely drawing attention to the real difficulties of those who see no purpose immanent in existence and have to choose it for themselves: admittedly useful to those who think that the satisfaction of current whim is the highest good. I do not think it a criticism of the play that it provides no solution to these difficulties.

KF: You make an interesting comment about time and meaning. And although time is a significant theme throughout 'Godot', I would have liked to see Beckett also highlight one of

the most complex theological problems there is: God's relationship with time and eternity. It's certainly more complex than
theodicy, though less emotional. Although characters in the
play suffer greatly, work on theodicy has over the past 35 years
made enormous progress. World leading philosophers Alvin
Plantinga, Peter van Inwagen and Paul Copan, to name but a
few, have all tackled reasonably well the problem of both moral
and natural evil. And although 'Godot' pre-dates them all, surely a scholar like Beckett would've read Aquinas or Augustine?
Even though we are discussing a literary and not a philosophical treatise, it's difficult to avoid the issue in such a profound
philosophical play infused with time and being. The main characters in 'Godot', like most properly basic Christians and New
Atheists, have a sophomoric perception of God. Vladimir and
Estragon's discussions of Scripture are trivial; almost childlike.
One wonders if they even believe in God. They are also finite
earthly beings and one day their 'time will be up'. But God is
eternal, with no cause, beginning or end. In a play about two
main characters struggling to cope by passing away the time on
earth, in Hell there is no exit; no Godot; no camaraderie or end.
But for Becket, there is no Hell as death ends at the grave, thus
relieving Vladimir and Estragon of the 'burden' of living. For
the Christian, however, belief in Hell is real. It is the terror of all
terrors: separation from God for eternity.

CHAPTER ELEVEN

The Catcher in the Rye
When disillusionment, alienation
and dysfunction become virtues
Kenneth Francis

I HAVE OFTEN WONDERED whether the American novel, *The Catcher in the Rye*, is a literary hoax, a kind of Leftist propaganda manifesto, manufactured to discredit traditional family values. And is it not coincidental that the Leftist generations after its post-1950s publication, were generally disaffected, drug-addled American youth who had become spiritually poisoned during the sexual revolution by a Godless culture culminating decades later in glorifying a toxic entertainment industry with vile lyrics and vulgar role models?

However, despite this, by today's standards of 'literature', the *Catcher* seems quite tame. This world-wide bestseller, which is a first-person narrative, seems to promote alienation and nihilism, as well as being devoid of wholesome values, is also quite bland and overrated. But criticism of this 'bible of teenage angst' amongst the 'Intelligentsia' is considered taboo; a kind of Emperor's New Prose for the 'chattering classes'.

The plot centres around a dull, vulgar, teenage phony boy furious with traditional family adult 'phonies'. It's a book written in 1951 by a recluse called J.D. Salinger, who avoided all media attention and disappeared from public life before he died over fifty years after the book was published, along with several other less-popular works penned by him.

The antihero of the book, 17-year-old Holden Caulfield, seems to be unaware that all teenagers and adults are not 100% perfect and have some disappointments and suffering in their lives in this fallen world. Much of this strife is self-inflicted, while some of it is not. However, he criticises adults but rarely reflects on his own obnoxious behaviour, despite wanting to become an adult himself.

But the book, unfortunately, has become infamous for some other strange reasons. When the ex-Beatle John Lennon was walking back to his New York apartment in the winter of 1980, he was stopped by a young male fan who asked him to sign an autograph. Sometime after Lennon signed the autograph, the man fatally shot the ex-Beatle five times. Soon after the incident and before his arrest, it is believed he sat down on the sidewalk beside the Dakota Apartments in New York City and started to read a copy of *The Catcher in the Rye*.

Many believe the fan, Mark Chapman, was 'inspired' by the book's main character, Holden Caulfield, when he murdered Lennon (there are also a couple of other incidents with loner assassins carrying the book). So, who exactly is this Holden character? In the book, he comes across to an intelligent reader as a kind of anti-hero for confused, rebellious youth.

The title of the book refers to a fantasy he has, where he watches and protects thousands of little children playing some game in a big field of rye. While they play, he stands all day at the edge of the field's cliff, making sure none of them fall off (a kind of metaphor for saving kids' innocence from the 'evils' of phoney adults). Did Chapman, who once idolised Lennon, think the ex-Beatle was really a phoney deep down? Shortly before his death, Lennon spoke in interviews in which he gave the impression he privately held many conservative views, despite his public, Leftist persona.

But it wasn't just Chapman who was allegedly 'inspired' by

the book. In America, *The Catcher in the Rye* quickly became the bible of teenage angst and alienation; a kind of Sartre for basement-dwelling, man-boys. And for decades, the book was forced on innocent students by numerous public high-school Marxist teachers. Think about it: a story about a nihilist loser who flunks boarding school and messes up as much as he can on his way home. A rebel without a brain, if you will. But you won't hear that from the leftist academia or media.

They view Holden as someone concerned about humanity. They'll never mention that he's a narcissistic, vulgar, dysfunctional, highly emotional, inwardly nasty cynic who seems to view almost everyone with contempt. Despite all this, he fantasises about catching little children who wander too close to the cliff's edge. Is this not a kind of personification of the Nanny State?

In his book *God in the Dock (Essays on Theology)*, C.S. Lewis said: 'Of all tyrannies, a tyranny exercised for the good of its victims may be the most oppressive. It may be better to live under robber barons than under omnipotent moral busybodies. The robber baron's cruelty may sometimes sleep, his cupidity may at some point be satiated; but those who torment us for our own good will torment us without end, for they do so with the approval of their consciences.'

And there's nothing worse than a State with an overactive conscience. Like an over-conscientious farmer, who wants the best for his livestock before they end up butchered in the slaughterhouse. Wearing a deer hunter's cap, which he describes as a 'people shooting hat,' Holden seems at peace in the museum, possibly judging exhibits who can't judge him.

Isn't it strange that Salinger, who wrote this frequently censored, anti-family, blasphemous, rebellious, violent, promiscuous, pro-smoking/drinking/lying book, became a recluse? Was the cliff in the rye field an imaginary threat, where 'little children' must be protected by their Big Brother? A generation of brainwashed sheep kept in line by a 'good' shepherd? Or is the story an autobiographical psychological projection of Salinger's world view? Was he a Marxist? Perhaps we'll never know.

Despite capitalism and economics not being a main feature in the book, the Italian Marxist Antonio Gramsci (1891-1937) said that to attain political power, the transforming of culture was of paramount importance. That's why Communist countries have Ministries for Culture. And there is no better way to transform culture than by books, the media, music, TV, movies and other types of entertainment.

In his Broadcast talk in June 1935, G.K. Chesterton said: 'The free man owns himself. He can damage himself with either eating or drinking; he can ruin himself with gambling. If he does he is certainly a damn fool, and he might possibly be a damned soul; but if he may not, he is not a free man any more than a dog.'

There's something sociopathic and sinister about *Catcher in the Rye*. How is it that this book is embraced by generations of students who feel alienated? America today has tens of thousands of Holdens who refuse to grow up.

The writer Robin Marantz Henig said: 'Young people are occupying a lot of our attention these days. They're suffering under student debt at greater rates than ever before, and they're experiencing unemployment at greater rates than the rest of the population, so everybody is very concerned. You're also hearing a lot about them living in their parents' basements, being slackers, never being able to grow up.'[1]

During the early 1950s, America, although not perfect, went through a kind of golden era in both education and social life. The most popular TV show (probably to get us hooked on the new propaganda medium) was 'Father Knows Best'. Imagine the outrage if a show like that was aired today (more likely it would be called, 'Patriarchal Rapist Knows Worst'!). Yes, things have changed dramatically. Today's Holdens and the rest of us are all lost in our sins (Psalm 51:5) and weaknesses in some way or other, alienated from God and in need of reconciliation.

---

1 'Why Millennials Aren't Growing Up', Robin Marantz Henig in an interview with Monica Williams, *U.S. News* (December 20, 2012).

CHAPTER TWELVE

Ionesco's *Le Roi Se Meurt* (*The King Departs*)
Theodore Dalrymple

ACCORDING TO HIS REMINISCENCES (which like all reminiscences may be a later elaboration to put some kind of retrospective order in a life), Eugène Ionesco was preoccupied with death from a very early age. He was, as it were, an infant prodigy of the fear of death. If death were the end of all, what larger meaning could be attached to life, and if there were no such larger meaning, how and why should we live?

Whether or not Ionesco's reminiscences were the literal truth about his early state of mind, the play of his that I consider his greatest, *Le Roi Se Meurt*, usually translated as *The King Departs*, is an extremely powerful depiction and exploration of the predicament of a man who does not believe in any kind of transcendence or continuing life after death.

The play, a long single scene, takes place in the crumbling palace (indistinguishable from a suburban home) of King Bérenger the First, whose kingdom has likewise crumbled during his reign so that it now covers only a very small territory with very few inhabitants, the only children left being cretins, hydrocephalics, and other assorted mentally handicapped.

The play, in my view the masterpiece of the so-called Theatre of the Absurd, opens with a discussion about the way in which Bérenger must be told that he is to die by the end of the production, that is to say in an hour and a half's time. The discussion takes place between his first Queen, Marguerite, his second Queen, Marie (who detest one another), and the Royal Physician, also the Royal Astrologer and Executioner, with interjections from Juliette, the Royal Nurse and Cleaning Lady, and the Guard.

The King is ill-prepared for the news of his impending demise. He can hardly move without pain, but first he denies and then dismisses the significance of the pain. When Marie says to him that he is limping, he replies, 'Limping? I'm not limping. I'm limping a little.'

Marguerite, his first Queen, says to him, 'Sire, we are obliged to tell you that you're going to die.' The Royal Physician confirms it: 'Alas, yes, Majesty.' The King replies, 'Yes, I know that of course. We all know it. Remind me when it's time...'

His entourage insists and tells him once more that he is going to die, without specifying exactly when. Bérenger (somehow a ridiculous name for a king) replies, 'What, again? You're boring me! I will die, yes, I will die. In forty years, in fifty, in three hundred. Later. When I would like to, when I will have the time, when I will decide.'

The play, first performed in 1962, captures perfectly the modern man's feeling that everything, including death, ought to be under his control, his refusal to accept existential limits that he has not imposed himself. And this, of course, makes him fearful and resentful in the face of those limits which, in the last analysis, are not his to control.

When his entourage tells him that he is going to die by the end of the play. He replies, 'Who has given these orders without my consent? I feel perfectly well. You've got a cheek! Lies. (To Marguerite.) You have always wanted me dead. (To Marie.) She has always wanted me dead. (To Marguerite.) I will die when I want, I am the King, it is I who decide.'

This little passage captures very precisely the strange predicament of modern man – which, incidentally, Ionesco himself shared, and is perhaps why he is able to capture it so precisely and so succinctly.

Modern man likes to believe himself rational to a degree unprecedented in history: but Man remains Man, and the King shows himself almost at one with the Azande, the Sudanese tribe as described by the social anthropologist, E. E. Evans-Pritchard, who believe that no one dies except by the malevolent magic performed by his enemies. And then he re-iterates that death is under his control.

Bérenger's kingship is purely symbolic: in reality he is Everyman, no one in fact more so. But we live in an age when each man considers himself King, with absolute sovereignty over himself. It is therefore up to him to decide not only when, but even whether, he dies, with the result that illness and death are regarded not as fatalities, in the sense of being at some time or other an inevitable consequence of having lived, but as injustices, or an infringement of rights. This feeling is transferred to loved ones, whose death is likewise not accepted: if someone dies, someone else must have failed to do what he ought to have done.

Bérenger complains first that no one ever told him he was close to death, and second that he is not ready, in the sense of being prepared, to die. This, of course, suggests that the *ars moriendi*, the art of dying, has been lost, precisely because we treat death as if it were an optional extra, like tinted windows in a car. Bérenger wants more time to prepare for death, as if what he wants could affect the matter. Marguerite says, 'At fifty, you wanted to wait for your sixties [to prepare]. You have had your sixtieth birthday, your ninetieth, your hundred and twenty-fifth, your four hundredth. You didn't put off your preparations any more for ten years, but for fifty. And now it's from century to century.'

To this the King replies, 'I really intended to start. Ah! If I could only have a century before me, perhaps I would have the time!' The Royal Physician interjects, 'You have only a little more than an hour left. Everything must be done within an hour.' Marie, his second Queen, who is not so much tender towards him as sentimental, says, 'He won't have time, it's not possible. He must have more time.' Marguerite, who has the hardness of the discarded, says, 'That's just what is impossible. But an hour, that's more than enough.'

That it is not a question of time alone, but of philosophical outlook, is suggested by what the Royal Physician says: 'An hour well employed is better than centuries and centuries of negligence and forgetfulness. Five minutes suffice, ten seconds of real consciousness. We have given him an hour: sixty minutes, three thousand six hundred seconds. He's lucky.'

Marguerite, disdainful of her former's husband's fear in the face of death, says, 'He imagines he's the first to die,' to which Marie replies, 'Everyone is the first to die.' This brings perfectly to light the inexpungible difference between knowledge by theory and observation, and that by personal experience. Neither is false, neither is the whole truth.

Marie tries to comfort Bérenger with the old Stoic argument about death: 'While death is still not there, you exist. When it is there, you will not be, so you will not meet it, you will not see it.' Marguerite, ever vengeful, says vehemently, 'The lies about life, the old sophisms! We are familiar with them all. Death has always been there, present from the first day, from conception. It is the shoot that grows, the flower that blooms, the only fruit.' In the midst of life, we are in death.

Supposedly consolatory efforts to get Bérenger to remember what it was like not to have existed, because that will be what it is like when he is dead, do not help him: he comes up against the Cartesian cogito. Non-existence is not a kind of highly attenuated experience, it is non-experience, and one cannot experience non-experience. The attempt to make him think that non-existence is a homeland therefore fails to console him.

The King asks the Royal Nurse and Cleaning Lady how she lives (now that he is dying, it is the first time that he ever has thought to ask, Marguerite saying that it doesn't really interest him, the Royal Physician adding that he is trying to buy time). 'I live badly,' replies the Royal Cleaning Lady, to which the King says, 'One cannot live badly, that is a contradiction.' In the face of death, but only in the face of death meaning extinction, life is appreciated as good in itself, irrespective of its content. The Royal Cleaning Lady enumerates all the respects in which she is obliged to live badly, but all these respects seem a sheer delight to someone like the King who is about to die.

When he says that he has nothing to comfort him, his entourage advises him to learn serenity, indifference and resignation, and invoke memories, that is to say 'memories of memories of memories' (a line that calls into question the relationship of memory to reality) to help assuage him. The palace Guard then prays for assistance: 'O Great Nothing, help the King.'

This is the ultimate absurdity, of course: to pray for assistance from nothingness, as if nothingness were not only something, but the kind of something that could take pity on a man and come to his succour.

At the end of the play, by Ionesco's express direction, the stage is left with nothing visible except a grey luminescence.

CHAPTER THIRTEEN

Ionesco's *The Lesson*
'Man is born unto trouble, as the sparks fly upward'
Kenneth Francis

THROUGHOUT MY PART-TIME LECTURING CAREER, I've
been lucky to work for fine institutions of learning.
However, the same can't be said of the growing number of 'bad
apples' in Western higher education. Theologian Peter Mullen,
writing in the *Salisbury Review* in 2017, said: 'Give me fifty
years of comprehensive education and I will show you a nation
of idiots.' According to Mr Mullen, the Department of Education (UK) itself admits that, after eleven years of compulsory
state education, 43% of pupils leave school unable to read, write
and count efficiently. 'Worse, two generations of teachers – who
come out with such expressions as "I was sat" and "I was stood"–
have gone through this system, so the result is dumber...'

However, not all schools or universities are bad. But ever
since the widespread use of social media and the rise of political
correctness, many institutions of education seem to have low-
ered their standards. Generation Selfie, particularly millennial
college students, live in an era of sound-bites, 'micro-aggres-
sions', 'safe spaces' and shallow, trolling tweets. Many students

in the Humanities, especially in the USA, are now chanting to ban free speech, closing down university buildings and rioting on the streets, physically attacking anyone in favour of free speech.

Aside from the good universities, this is what happens when places of education become factories for the indoctrination of sensitivity fascists, encouraging them to oppose free speech, truth, and the concept of reality. God help any student in such an institution who is rational, fair-minded, moral and in search of truth; or worse: a White Christian male wanting to date a girl to be his future wife and mother of his children.

In this Theatre-of-the-Absurd Soviet gulag, identity politics, victimhood and political correctness rule with a metaphorical taser gun inside a velvet glove, and any dissenters of ridiculous false propositions risk being ridiculed, ostracised or treated with contempt.

In *Taki's Magazine* in May 2017, Theodore Dalrymple hits the nail on the head regarding the West's subtle transition into Sovietization without a revolution or a single bullet being fired: 'For to force people to assent to propositions that are outrageously false, on pain of losing their livelihoods or worse, was to crush them morally and psychologically, and thus make them docile, easily manipulated, and complicit in their own enslavement.'

This enslavement goes back to the foot of the Cross on Calvary. By rejecting Christ, we reject Logos: Logic, Reason and Truth. The whole objective moral order rests on this. But in 21st century higher education, Postmodernism is evident, even in some popular dramas.

An Absurdist play called *The Lesson*, which premiered in Paris in 1951, has parallels with some contemporary higher education. It was written by Eugene Ionesco (1909-1994) who was of Romanian origin but his writings are predominantly French. The success of this one-act play is evident even today in Paris, where on a regular basis it can still be seen in Left Bank theatres due to its great contribution to the avant-garde, Theatre-of-the-Absurd genre.

Like most Absurdist dramatists, Ionesco was reluctant to theorise about his work. However, *The Lesson* is certainly a play worth theorising about in the context of today's decline in education and absurd teaching ideology. The scene is simple: an office and dining-room of a cosy flat where a fifty-something Professor works. His maid is a middle-aged woman, and they are joined by an 18-year-old female Pupil who arrives for a lesson.

Although the Professor is not intentionally of the Marxist, pony-tailed type, he nonetheless has much in common ideologically with the totalitarian, Maoist leftists of contemporary Western gagademia. Throughout the absurd lesson, the Professor grows agitated with the Pupil, with what he sees are her ignorant answers to his quirky, infantile questions.

She gradually becomes nervous, subdued and is psychologically broken by the Professor's later aggressive tone. He eventually stabs and murders the Pupil near the end of the play, to which the Maid greets a new pupil, thus potentially repeating the crazy cycle.

To explore this further, let us return to the Whacky World of Western Gagademia. Here in the early decades of the 21st century, tragedy, bleakness and farce haunt the secular corridors of many, not all, Humanities departments of higher education. The tenure-obsessed, high-priest professors here have a lot in common with the Professor when it comes to absurdity.

These academics may not be murderers, but their Postmodern lessons of indoctrination would give the mad Lesson's Professor a run for his money. Writing in the *Brussels Journal* in 2015, English professor Thomas F. Bertonneau said: 'Modern education, including modern higher education, not only denies the existence of truth while obfuscating the difference between ignorance and knowledge; it also rejects the past as unworthy of study except in limited, prescriptive ways, as an object of ridicule or execration.

'The English departments of the USA's colleges and universities now focus almost entirely on contemporary rather than historical material – one may graduate with a baccalaureate in English Literature from numerous colleges and universities without having read Chaucer, Shakespeare, George Eliot, or Henry James, all of whom have become optional where they have not disappeared altogether from the reading-list.'

Furthermore, many Humanities campuses are notoriously devoted to radical Feminism, racism (often used as a code word for anti-White) and gender issues. The writer Jim Goad says that American education these days is not to fill minds with new ideas, but to cleanse them of all unacceptable ideas, no matter how logical, natural, and instinctual those ideas may be. 'From preschool all the way through to grad school, American academia is no longer a world of education, but of indoctrination,' he wrote in *Taki's Magazine* in 2016.

And it won't be long before some STEM lessons will also be corrupted by the Postmodern language of the progressives. After all, it is the 'evil' White Christian bourgeoisie who uphold logic and reason. Like the dysfunctional lesson taught by the Professor to the Pupil, the modern-day equivalent seeks to break-up the Divine Order, in favour of the decadent, and instead teach obscenities. Here, Darwinism and Marxism (I'll exclude Nietzscheism because of his brute honesty and anti-egalitarian views) are the order of the day to degrade rather than uplift and empower the soul.

Vulgarity and stupidity are praised, while decency and sophisticated behaviour are derided or ridiculed. But back to *The Lesson*: The Pupil is clueless, yet she has high aspirations of academic achievements and success beyond her infantile intellect (sound familiar?) And the Professor is domineering and a bully-turned-murderer, similar to the many Marxist deranged murderers of high culture in today's campuses. Many critics have interpreted *The Lesson* as a response to Nazi activity in France during the Second World War. If the young Ionesco witnessed such activities while living in France as a young man, it's possible he used the bullying aspects as themes to his subsequent literature. Back to the play:

PUPIL: '... I'm lucky, my parents aren't badly off. They'll be able to help me in my work, so that I can take the highest degrees there are.'

PROFESSOR: '...You are most knowledgeable already. And so young, too...'

The Pupil is anything but bright but this is the world of the Absurd Theatre so it doesn't matter if he is right or wrong or she is bright or stupid. It's likewise in some contemporary institutions, where truth dies a thousand deaths and what feels right is all that matters.

PROFESSOR: 'What do one and one make?'

PUPIL: 'One and one make two.'

PROFESSOR: [astounded by his pupil's erudition]: 'But that's very good indeed! You're extremely advanced in your studies. You'll have very little difficult in passing all your doctorate examinations.'

Who would've ever imagined back in the 1950s that an Absurdist play would have parallels with reality in 60 years' time? A world where proficiently in arithmetic is declining. Many factors could take the blame from digital calculators to rote learning replacing discovery-based methods promoting multiple strategies and estimations, not to mention affirmative action. Switching from arithmetic to philology, the Professor begins to show signs of schizophrenia as his earlier mild engagement with the Pupil becomes aggressive.

PROFESSOR: '...How, for example, would you say, in English, the roses of my grandmother are as yellow as my grandmother who was born in Asia?'

PUPIL: [Who has a toothache] 'Toothache! Toothache! Toothache!"

PROFESSOR: 'Come along now, that doesn't stop you saying it!'

PUPIL: 'In English?'

PROFESSOR: 'In English.'

English for the Millennials, especially students, is not anything to 'LOL' about or 'GR8'. Even grammar and proper English are in decline, with many words becoming bastardized. But why should writing proper English matter when lessons on identity politics and gender seem to be all that matters?

Criminology professor Mike Adams is no stranger to the madness that passes for higher education in the corridors of American academia. Adams, who is a Christian and lectures at the University of North Carolina Wilmington, is also the author of *Letters To A Young Progressive: How To Stop Wasting Your Life Protesting Things You Don't Understand.* He once referred to higher education in his country as Theatre of the Absurd. And he was called by some of his colleagues 'the biggest embarrassment to higher education in America'.[1]

If you think Ionesco's *Lesson* is absurd, then consider what facts Adams replied with on being called an embarrassment: First, in the early spring semester of 2013, a women's studies professor and a psychology professor at Western Carolina University co-sponsored a panel on bondage and S&M. At Duke University, feminists hired a "sex worker" to speak as part of an event called the Sex Workers Art Show. After his speech, the male prostitute pulled down his pants, got down on his knees, and inserted a burning sparkler into his rectum. While it burned, he sang a verse of 'The Star Spangled Banner'. This brings a new meaning to Job 5:7: 'Yet man is born unto trouble, as the sparks fly upward'.

But it's not just the University of North Carolina that featured such cultural gems. Harvard University hosted an anal sex workshop teaching students how to 'put things in your butt'.

1 Mike Adams, *ClashDaily*, August 28, 2013.

Around 50 students attended, according to college paper, *The College Fix,* to learn how to stimulate nerves in the rectum, how to use anal beads, and how to avoid infections, according to the *Daily Mail* in 2017. It is the second time the university has held a talk on anal sex, instead of practical life skills in education; the first was in 2014. There were more incidents but it's obvious Ionesco's *Lesson* is no match for the above campus lunacy when it comes to absurdity. But this lunacy isn't a new phenomenon. Back in 1948, W. H. Auden, writing in *The New Yorker* in July of that year, said: 'As long as employers demand a degree for jobs to which a degree is irrelevant, the colleges will be swamped by students who have no disinterested love of knowledge, and teachers, particularly in the Humanities, aware of the students' economic need to pass examinations, will lower their standards to let them.'

In a book highly critical of the American education system, the authors Samuel Blumenfeld and Alex Newman, wrote: 'How many parents ... send their children to school so central planners can mold them into functionally illiterate cogs in a centrally planned machine, having just enough knowledge to do their preassigned task? How will such cogs be able to think critically, much less sustain liberty and the American experiment? The short answer is that they will not – and that is the point.'[2]

When Ionesco said without God, all actions become senseless, absurd, useless, he was right.[3] It's easy to see how the absurd crept into some sections of academia with the anti-Christian influence of radical atheists like the Frankfurt School. As in most Absurdist drama, the characters in *The Lesson* just seem to be going through the motions without any reference to Man's Divine Creator.

Look at many young students today and see the similarity. They wear victimhood on their sleeves like badges of honour

2 Samuel Blumenfeld and Alex Newman, *Crimes of the Educators: How Untopians Are Using Government Schools to Destroy America's Children*, WND Books (2015).

3 Eugene Ionesco, *Dans les armes de la ville*, Cahiers de la Compagnie Madeleine Renaud-Jean-Louis Barrault, Paris, No. 20, October 1957.

and appear zombie-like, dysfunctional and alienated from each other. Some behave like animals because they are told we are all animals, thus Darwin is their god.

The drama of Theatre of the Absurd could now morph into conventional theatre in a world where bitter is sweet, dark is light, and evil is good. A world where God is denied or blasphemed; a place where those trapped in their mental servility of narcissism and entitlement reject all that is absolute, virtuous, truthful, beautiful and transcendental. Like the world of *The Lesson*, modern Man/Woman without God is also trapped in a world of illusory unreality without foundations.

Many students might not be physically murdered by the teachings of their professors, but the metaphorical knife 'still goes in', killing the spirit of Truth and Reality. And the ultimate knife used to weaponize language is through the new PC liberalism. But it wasn't always that way.

According to American academic and social critic Camille Paglia: 'Liberalism of the 1950s and '60s exalted civil liberties, individualism, and dissident thought and speech. "Question authority" was our generation rubric when I was in college.

'But today's liberalism has become grotesquely mechanistic and authoritarian. It's all about reducing individuals to a group identity, defining that group in permanent victim terms, and denying others their democratic right to challenge that group and its ideology. Political correctness represents the fossilized institutionalisation of once-vital revolutionary ideas, which have become mere formulas.' Paglia says this is repressively Stalinist, dependent on a 'labyrinthine, parasitic bureaucracy to enforce its empty dictates.'[4]

In George Orwell's *Nineteen Eighty Four*,[5] the protagonist Winston is tied to a bed being tortured by Party member, O'Brien, who holds up four fingers and asks: 'How many am I holding up?' When Winston answers 'four', O'Brien says, 'no, I'm holding up five'; he then electrocutes Winston.

---

4 Camille Paglia, 'On Trump, Democrats, Transgenderism, and Islamist Terror', *The Weekly Standard* (June 15, 2017).

5 George Orwell, *Nineteen Eighty Four*, Secker & Warburg (1949).

O'Brien continues this until the atheist Winston eventually answers, 'five'.

Like Ionesco's Pupil, Winston and the other Godless state slaves' psychological make-up have become passive and disoriented in the anti-Logos 'learning' factories of the Secular West. With a pupil spiritually murdered by atheistic indoctrination, another pupil knocks on the door of academia in preparation for their lesson. In the Theatre of the Absurd, the lesson of *The Lesson* is in the words of the Professor after he murders his Pupil: '...What will come of it all? Oh, dear, oh, dear! How awful...'

CHAPTER FOURTEEN

Philip Larkin's 'Aubade'
Theodore Dalrymple

PESSIMISTS, I HAVE NOTICED, are better company than optimists. Is there such a thing, indeed, as an optimistic joke? There is practically nothing duller in life than to listen to an optimist outlining the glorious, happy future that is about to envelop us all.

Pessimists see the cloud in every silver lining and usually – no, *always* – they are right. Man, said the Russian writer V. G. Korolenko, is made for happiness: in which case, worms were made for flight.

Pessimists come in different shapes, sizes and degrees of course; and if it is almost impossible to conceive of humour without pessimism, at least humour of any subtlety, it does not follow that all pessimists are humorous. Nevertheless, to adapt very slightly Keats' great lines:

Aye, in the very temple of melancholy
Veil'd humour has her sovereign shrine.

Philip Larkin was a man of the deepest-dyed pessimism who had an acid sense of humour and (much rarer) a great poetic gift. Whether a man chooses a philosophy or a philosophy chooses a man is a matter of debate, as is the degree to which

Larkin's pessimism was the result or cause of his experiences.

Let us just say, to avoid being too categorical, that the relationship was dialectical. He himself put it well:

> Strange reciprocity:
> The circumstance we cause
> In time gives rise to us,
> Becomes our memory.

Perhaps we should add for completeness' sake that, born in 1922, he certainly grew up in times propitious for pessimism.

He was, of course, quite without religious belief. Death for him was final and life without transcendent purpose or meaning: it was a brief interval of consciousness between two eternities of non-being. He and we can never know if he was right because, if he were right, there would be no subject to know it.

It is on these grounds that the Stoics denied that death was to be feared, at least not as a state (of course, the process of dying, more often than not a very unpleasant one, is to be feared, but that is because the subject of the process is still alive to experience it). The Stoics may have it in logic – assuming, that is, that there really is no after-life – but somehow the logic brings no comfort even to those who assent to it. The reasoning has something of whistling in the wind about it, which mere argumentation cannot dispel: for the heart has its reasons that reason knows not of. And the prospect of future non-being, now that we have been, so to speak, cannot strike us in the same way, or with the same indifference, as past non-being. At least, I speak of the great majority of men the great majority of the time.

Philip Larkin was not one of those men who could comfort themselves with rational thoughts about the prospect of non-being. He too raged, raged against the dying of the light. His poem 'Aubade' (an aubade is a song or musical piece to be sung or played at the dawning of the day) is a *cri de coeur* against his own approaching dissolution. In fact, he was not a long-lived man: when he wrote this poem, he had only seven years to live and died aged 63. Compared with eternity, a few more years might seem insignificant, but compared with the period granted to human life a great deal. Death was always much, one might say enormously, on Larkin's mind.

The opening lines set the scene and the tone:

> I work all day, and get half-drunk at night.
> Waking at four to soundless dark, I stare.

The psychiatrist of today thinks, aha, early-morning waking, time for an anti-depressant. But does he drink because he is depressed, or is he depressed because he drinks? (Alcohol puts you to sleep, but interferes with the quality of sleep thereafter, as I know only too well.)

But the problem is – if one may be permitted so pretentious a word – existential:

> In time the curtain-edges will grow light.
> Till then I see what's really always there:
> Unresting death, a whole day nearer now...

Twenty-three years earlier, he had protested not against death, but against work:

> Why should I let the toad work
> Squat on my life?

Work dominates his existence:

> Six days of the week it soils
> With its sickening poison –
> Just for paying a few bills!
> That's out of proportion.

Eight years later, he revises his attitude to work. This is not because he actually likes work, finds it uplifting or worthwhile in itself, but because it's better than the alternative, which is to wander aimlessly, pathetically in the park because of incapacity of one kind or another:

All dodging the toad work
By being stupid or weak.
Think of being them!
Hearing the hours chime…

At least if you work you are not one of them. Work isn't to pay your bills any more, it is to pass the time without becoming one of them. This is a pretty bleak view of the possibilities of human existence, and one cannot help but wonder whether it is better to have been disillusioned than never to have been illusioned at all? (Even at my age, six years older than Larkin when he died, I think of whatever work I am engaged upon as being important, though I know perfectly that it will make no difference to anyone, at least not for more than a few seconds.) Work is a prop to help Larkin get though life. Rather than idleness, he says:

… give me my in-tray,
My loaf-haired secretary,
My shall-I-keep-the-call-in-Sir:
What else can I answer,

When the lights come on at four
At the end of another year?
Give me your arm, old toad;
Help me down Cemetery Road.

This was written twenty-three years before Larkin's death, an interval that I can remember thinking, and not so very long ago, was very long, but which now seems to me a mere blinking of the eye. At Larkin's age when he wrote about his progress down Cemetery Road, I was certainly not as aware of, or as concerned by, death as he; indeed, I was still courting danger as if it could not possibly apply to me, as if I were indestructible and in effect immortal. I look back and think that I was frivolous: and yet, if everyone had a Larkin-like awareness of the proximity of death, a subject that in some moods I feel is the only one worth thinking about, in so far as it is death that gives meaning, or at least impulsion, to life, no one would ever do anything. Without the illusion that something matters, and matters beyond the compass of our own lives, we should be doomed to – well, what exactly? Life has its imperatives that no philosophy can annul. And in fact Larkin himself worked diligently and successfully for many years as Librarian to Hull University. He did not find the work pointless because he was soon to die, as were all those whom he served directly or indirectly.

This does not, of course, make him a hypocrite or a humbug (of hypocrisy and humbuggery, the latter is far the worse). The mood of What's it all for? must surely take most of us at some time. That we cannot keep it up, that we must return before long to our normal avocations, does not mean that it was false or bogus or forced. And in some temperaments, the mood must come on more frequently than in others. A man who has never asked what is it all for, who has gone through life simply as an insurance loss adjustor, say (and by the way, a very interesting job if it means dealing personally with claimants), without ever asking what it is all for, is in a way a very dangerous man, the kind of man who would obey any orders.

But Larkin carries bleakness to a new pitch, if bleakness can be said to have a positive rather than a merely negative quality. Unresting death, as he calls it, makes all thought impossible (for him, be it remembered, but for all of us if we enter his world, as the poem surely does, such is its power), except:

> … where and when I shall myself die.
> This mode of thought, as he well knows, is futile:
> Arid interrogation: yet the dread
> Of dying, and being dead,
> Flashes afresh to hold and horrify.

Larkin does not allow himself any Stoic consolation, which I suspect he would have regarded as cheap, as if the Stoics were door-to-door salesmen selling death as a harmless product. No; it is the prospect of utter extinction that horrifies:

The mind blanks at the glare. Not in remorse...
But at the total emptiness for ever,
The sure extinction that we travel to
And shall be lost in always. Not to be here,
Not to be anywhere,
And soon; nothing more terrible, nothing more true.

I suspect that not many people can entirely free themselves from this thought, if they approach the subject at all. Some of Larkin's bleakness no doubt relates to his particular, and slightly peculiar, biography, for example in this poem written when he was fifty (no great age, as I now think):

Where has it gone, the lifetime?
Search me. What's left is drear.
Unchilded and unwifed, I'm
Able to view that clear:
So final. And so near.

But one cannot think of 'Aubade' as simply a manifestation of personal psychopathology: it poses a challenge to us all. And oddly enough, just as pessimism does not preclude humour but rather encourages or promotes it, so Larkin's poetry uplifts rather than depresses. It in some mysterious way which I cannot fully explain reconciles us to our condition, as only art can do.

CHAPTER FIFTEEN

Solzhenitsyn's
One Day in the Life of Ivan Denisovich
Mankind has forgotten God
Kenneth Francis

RUSSIAN LITERATURE is permeated with the themes of misery and war. And nowhere are such unimaginable horrors more prominent and terrifying than in the writings of Aleksandr Solzhenitsyn (1918-2008).

Nobel laureate, mathematician, Orthodox Christian author, and Russian dissident, he was a man who experienced first-hand the terror of existence when humans forget God. He was also an outspoken critic of the Soviet Union and the barbarism of atheistic totalitarianism. If he were alive today, he'd probably be cautiously optimistic for Mother Russia's future but pessimistic about the West.

Generation after generation, other great Russian writers like Tolstoy, Dostoevsky, Gogol and Pasternak have laid bare the turmoil, repression, poverty, death, sadness and suffering of the Russian people. But none are more graphic or memorable than those penned by Solzhenitsyn.

While serving in the Russian Army in 1945, he was arrested and sent to prison for criticizing, in a letter, the Russian leader

Josef Stalin. While in prison, Solzhenitsyn met Christians and was astonished at their deep faith in Christ and great strength in the harsh conditions of the gulag. It was then that he found God.

On release from prison and in exile, he was repulsed by the moral decadence of the West. However, in his most famous book and masterpiece, the non-fiction *The Gulag Archipelago*, he recalls the horrors of the Russian revolution and its aftermath (1918-1956). This madness led to tens of millions of innocent people being imprisoned in forced labour camps, tortured, diseased-ridden, raped, starved and executed by a regime that hated an entity they didn't even believe in: The God of Christianity, Jesus Christ.

This essay focuses on a speech by Solzhenitsyn, reflecting both his non-fiction work and his most-famous novel, *One Day in the Life of Ivan Denisovich*. Ivan Denisovich Shukhov has been sentenced to a camp in the Soviet gulag during World War Two. He is accused of becoming a spy, which he's not, and is sentenced to ten years in a forced labor camp. The story chronicles Ivan's day-to-day life in the squalor of the prison camp, where fellow prisoners are treated with some compassion, but mainly harshly and with cruelty in freezing conditions.

Here, survival of the fittest is exercised throughout the prison camp. The theme of the story is totalitarian oppression and survival. In his Templeton Address in London on May 10, 1983, that laid bare the evil some humans do when God is proclaimed dead, Solzhenitsyn said:

> . . . If I were asked today to formulate as concisely as possible the main cause of the ruinous Revolution that swallowed up some sixty million of our people, I could not put it more accurately than to repeat: Men have forgotten God; that's why all this has happened.

In the West today, most visibly since the early-1960s, we see this happening at a rapid pace. Only this time, especially in the 21st century, it is a fascist brand of liberalism with a smiley face.

The Equality Police of the New Establishment, and their dedicated proxy warriors on the left, can make life hell for the Ivans of this world or any follower of Christ.

> The failings of human consciousness, deprived of its divine dimension, have been a determining factor in all the major crimes of this century . . . The only possible explanation for [these wars] is a mental eclipse among the leaders of Europe due to their lost awareness of a Supreme Power above them. Only a godless embitterment could have moved ostensibly Christian states to employ poison gas, a weapon so obviously beyond the limits of humanity.

In a deterministic universe without a divine dimension, we are nothing more than a pack of hungry hyenas feeding off a dead zebra. Do hyenas reform their gourmet preferences toward rotten carrion? Moral evil involves a conscious decision by a moral agent to engage in such vile atrocities of employing poison gas to vaporise the innocent. But the Big Bang of Naturalism has determined everything and all actions would be mere echoes of such a cataclysmic event. However, the Big Bang, if created by God, gives us freedom of the will.

> The same kind of defect, the flaw of a consciousness lacking all divine dimension, was manifested after World War II when the West yielded to the satanic temptation of the 'nuclear umbrella.' It was equivalent to saying: Let's cast off worries, let's free the younger generation from their duties and obligations, let's make no effort to defend ourselves, to say nothing of defending others - let's stop our ears to the groans emanating from the East, and let us live instead in the pursuit of happiness.

Satanic temptation is real. To say such supernatural evil doesn't exist is to say that millions of humans being vaporised by a nuclear bomb is nothing more than the rearrangement of atoms. Shielding our ears from the groans emanating from Western or Eastern holocausts in the pursuit of happiness is evil and satanic.

Isn't it strange that since many young people have forgotten God, cast off their worries and freed themselves from their duties and obligations, the moral decay and decadence of the West and beyond continue to intensify? And from the strange to the bizarre that people recently wept for joy and partied into the night when abortion was made legal in two formerly religious countries?

As for the pursuit of happiness: serial killers, psychopaths and ruthless corporate sociopaths follow this mantra with gusto to the detriment of the victims they swat-out and stamp on along the way in order to obtain relativistic, moral bliss. But you won't find such evil on their social media profiles, where 'human rights', 'child protection', 'equality' and 'tolerance' are amongst their many phoney virtue-signalling causes. It's gotten to the stage that they're stoned on virtue and don't understand Truth or the concept of God. What would Solzhenitsyn think of today's world, more than three decades after his speech?

> Today's [1983] world has reached a stage which, if it had been described to preceding centuries, would have called forth the cry: 'This is the Apocalypse!' Yet we have grown used to this kind of world; we even feel at home in it. Dostoevsky warned that 'great events could come upon us and catch us intellectually unprepared.' This is precisely what has happened. And he predicted that 'the world will be saved only after it has been possessed by the demon of evil.

The Bible also predicted this moral chaos. The above quote was written long before animal brothels for zoophiles ('erotic zoos') were introduced in some Western countries; before female prostitute robots were made available to men; before aborted babies' body parts were being sold in the West. And you thought the Island of Doctor Moreau was macabre and morally sick?

> Whether it really will be saved we shall have to wait and see: this will depend on our conscience, on our spiritual lucidity, on our individual and combined efforts in the face of catastrophic circumstances. But it has already come to pass that the demon of evil, like a whirlwind, triumphantly circles all five continents of the earth.

In the Bible (John 12:31) it says: 'Now is the time for judgment on this world; now the prince of this world will be driven out.' In a fallen world ruled by Satan, Solzhenitsyn was all too familiar with the evil people do when rejecting Christ. That is not to say all atheists are bad. Many atheists are morally good people but it's difficult for them to justify their morality objectively.

As for the Christian, the Romanian writer Richard Wurmbrand (1909-2001), who was tortured for his faith in a Communist prison, wrote about the cruelty of atheism 'which is hard to believe when man has no faith in the reward of faith in the reward of good or the punishment of evil.'

Wurmbrand said, according to this worldview, there is no reason to be human, as there is no restraint from the depths of evil which is in man. He wrote: 'The Communist torturers often said, "There is no God. There is no hereafter. No punishment for evil. We can do what we wish!" I have even heard one torturer say, "I thank God in whom I don't believe that I have lived to this hour when I can express all of the evil in my heart." He expressed it in unbelievable brutality and torture inflicted on prisoners.'

Solzhenitsyn continues:

> By the time of the Revolution, faith had virtually disappeared in Russian educated circles; and amongst the uneducated, its health was threatened. In its past, Russia did know a time when the social ideal was not fame, or

riches, or material success, but a pious way of life. Russia was then steeped in an Orthodox Christianity which remained true to the Church of the first centuries.

Then in the 19th century, the path to Marxism was opened. By the time of the Revolution, faith had virtually disappeared in Russian educated circles; and amongst the uneducated, its health was threatened, according to Solzhenitsyn.

It was the great Existentialist Russian writer, Dostoevsky, who drew from the French Revolution and its hatred of the Church, the lesson that 'revolution must necessarily begin with atheism'.

Solzhenitsyn again:

> But the world had never before known a godlessness as organized, militarized, and tenaciously malevolent as that practiced by Marxism. *Within the philosophical system of Marx and Lenin, and at the heart of their psychology, hatred of God is the principal driving force,* more fundamental than all their political and economic pretensions. Militant atheism is not merely incidental or marginal to Communist policy; it is not a side effect, but the central pivot.

What followed was the stuff of nightmares. Thousands of churches were destroyed; tens of thousands of clergy were tortured, shot, sent to labour camps, dumped onto the streets, penniless, and exiled to the desolate regions of the freezing north. Solzhenitsyn said all of these Christian martyrs went unswervingly to their deaths for the faith; 'instances of apostasy were few and far between. For tens of millions of laymen, access to the Church was blocked, and they were forbidden to bring up their children in the Faith'. Religious parents had their children taken away from them and they were thrown into prison. And to think many leftists today wear T-shirts with the hammer-and-sickle image emblazoned on them.

But there is something they did not expect: that in a land where churches have been levelled, where a triumphant atheism has rampaged uncontrolled for two-thirds of a century, where the clergy is utterly humiliated and deprived of all independence, where what remains of the Church as an institution is tolerated only for the sake of propaganda directed at the West, where even today people are sent to the labour camps for their faith ... As is always the case in times of persecution and suffering, the awareness of God in my country has attained great acuteness and profundity.

In the decadent (anti-)West, where political persecution was relatively non-existent during the time of Solzhenitsyn's lecture, the great dissident quickly became a non-person. The liberal 'Intelligentsia' in the popular media 'don't do God', thus it was a great disappointment to see such a maverick proudly wear his Christianity on his sleeve. This was, and still is, the worst secular sin.

Over 30 years later, the same thing is happening to the Christian Russian leader Vladimir Putin. He said many Euro-Atlantic countries have moved away from their roots, including Christian values and that this is the path to degradation.

Some will point to Putin's KGB past as an example of him possibly lying, but many people's views, including Putin's, can change over the years. An example is the former KGB officer Yuri Bezmenov, who was a member of the elite propaganda arm of the Committee. After becoming disillusioned with the evil system, he risked his life by escaping to the West. Like Solzhenitsyn, he spoke about the evils of Communism.

He said: 'It takes from 15 to 20 years to demoralize a nation. Why that many years? Because this is the minimum number of years required to educate one generation of students in the country of your enemy exposed to the ideology of [their] enemy. In other words, Marxism-Leninism ideology is being pumped into the soft heads of at least three generations of American students without being challenged or counterbalanced by the basic values of Americanism; American patriotism.'

Like George Orwell, who also wrote about the evil of Communism in his most famous book, *Nineteen Eighty Four*, Bezmenov coincidently said these above words in an interview in 1984. As for Putin (who remains an enigma): he recently inaugurated an enormous statue of St. Vladimir, the patron saint of the Russian Orthodox Church, about 100 yards from the Kremlin walls.

Iben Thranholm, one of Denmark's most widely read columnists, says this of the statue: 'If you stand at a certain point across the street from the Kremlin, the cross that he bears is even taller than the star in the Red Square, so the symbolism is very potent. In the West... we are going the other way. We can't discard our values and heritage fast enough.'

Is it true that post-Soviet Russia has now morally and spiritually traded places with the West, especially the USA? The writer and magazine editor, Taki Theodoracopulos, says: 'Russians are a spiritual people who yearn to connect with Christ, not Wall Street.'

In a series of lectures, he gave at Wheaton College in Chicago in 1968, the theologian Francis Shaeffer said: 'We live in a post-Christian world . . . There is no exhibition of this anywhere in history so clearly in such a short expanse of years as in our own generation... Having turned away from the knowledge given by God, man has now lost the whole Christian culture.'

And to think he said this 50 years ago. What would he think now, had he lived to see today? A day when an abortion clinic official, having lunch, jokes about buying a Lamborghini if she gets the best price for some aborted baby's tissue and body parts.

And those who criticise such vile comments, have become the Ivan Denisovich's of our age: sentenced to career suicide and social exclusion in the PC gulag of no man's land: a metaphorical labor camp of isolation from 'respectable' Twitter circles or dinner party get-togethers. A mental place where fellow 'prisoners' are treated with zero compassion, but mainly harshly and with cruelty in freezing conditions. The gulag hasn't gone away, you know.

CHAPTER SIXTEEN

Shakespeare's Hamlet
Theodore Dalrymple

I T SEEMS TO ME, in my unsystematic and unscholarly way, that some of Shakespeare's plays contain lines that distil, as it were, what the play is about – assuming, that is, that complex works of literature can be said to be about anything that can be thus distilled.

The action of *King Lear*, for example, follows from the King's foolish decision to throw himself upon the mercy of his two daughters, Goneril and Regan, because of their extravagant professions of love for him, while disinheriting Cordelia because she makes no such profession. Kent warns Lear:

Nor are those empty hearted whose low sound
Reverbs no hollowness…

but Lear takes no notice and prefers to believe that words must mean what they say and necessarily reflect the true thoughts and feelings of those that utter them. The rest of the play is long, painful and tragic lesson that this is not so: a lesson that we (mankind) never learn once and for all.

In *Hamlet*, according to my method of distillation, the crucial lines come in the scene in which Guildenstern has been sent by the usurping king, Claudius, to find out from Hamlet what is bothering him and making him behave so strangely. Hamlet, of course, is fully aware of who has sent Guildenstern and what he is really up to.

Hamlet asks Guildenstern, 'Will you play upon this pipe?'

GUILDENSTERN: My lord, I cannot.

HAMLET: I pray you.

GUILDENSTERN: Believe me, I cannot.

HAMLET: I do beseech you.

GUILDRENSETRN: I know no touch of it my lord.

HAMLET: It is as easy as lying. Govern these ventages with your fingers and thumb, give it breath with your mouth, and it will discourse most eloquent music. Look you, these are the stops.

GUILDENSTERN: But these cannot I command to any utterance of harmony. I have not the skill.

HAMLET: Why, look you now, how unworthy a thing you make of me! You would play upon me. You would seem to know my stops. You would pluck out the heart of my mystery. You would sound me from my lowest note to the top of my compass. And there is much music, excellent voice, in this little organ, yet you cannot make it speak? 'Sblood, do you think I am easier to be played on than a pipe? Call me what instrument you will, though you can fret me, yet you cannot play upon me.

You would pluck out the heart of my mystery: you would seek to know my innermost thoughts and my most secret motives. Yet this is something that you cannot do and will never be able to do.

What, exactly, is the mystery whose heart Guildenstern would pluck out of Hamlet? Is it that Hamlet knows it himself and that it, the mystery, could be plucked out by, say, torture? That if Hamlet were put on the rack, eventually he would reveal his very essence to his torturer?

Such a procedure might get him to reveal some information about himself and his thoughts: but even then, the torturer could never be quite certain that what was revealed was true, or merely uttered to bring the torture to an end. No doubt also some information extracted thus could be verified: the whereabouts of such and such a person, for example. But this is not the kind of information that Guildenstern seeks, which is intrinsically ambiguous and doubtful. Even the North Korean regime cannot know what its citizens – or prisoners – are thinking; and despite the much-vaunted advances in neurosciences, I think it highly unlikely that this radical ignorance will ever be overcome, for example by a thought-scanning machine that will be able to print out a person's thoughts as he is having them. And even this would be insufficient, for we all have simultaneous layers of thoughts and emotions, of which we are to varying degrees aware. The very existence of such a machine, the mere possibility that it were being employed upon us, would alter the nature of our thoughts.

Guildenstern's efforts are not the first time in the play that an effort has been made to 'understand' Hamlet. Claudius' trusty courtier, Polonius (who, one suspects, would serve anyone faithfully to save his own position), tells the king that he knows the cause of Hamlet's distemper, namely a passion for his daughter, Ophelia. This, of course, leads to a fiasco: and Polonius' pretensions to understanding are exposed as what they are, mere pretensions.

Hamlet does not understand himself, and the more he thinks about it, the less he understands. When the players have come to Elsinore to distract him from his apparent melancholy, he asks them first to perform an extract from a play that he has previously seen them enact. When they have done so and have left Hamlet to himself, he recites one of his great soliloquies: *O what a peasant slave and rogue am I...*

In this speech, he draws attention – ours and his own – to the fact that, while he has every motive for heightened passion, namely a murdered father, a usurped kingdom, and a faithless mother, he cannot express it with the emotional force employed by the actors recounting imaginary events: *What's Hecuba to him, or he to Hecuba...* etc. His emotional confusion is complete.

What are Hamlet's true feelings for Ophelia? He treats her first with truly abominable, almost sadistic, cruelty: but when she dies he appears also to grieve immeasurably for her, and claims to have loved her more than thirty-thousand brothers ever could have done. Again, we cannot help but observe the contradictions in Hamlet's psyche, but we do not conclude that they arise from Shakespeare's incompetence as a dramatist, or from his inability to depict a coherent character. In a sense, Hamlet's incoherence is his coherence, and if we all spent as much time thinking about ourselves and our situation in the world, we should all be as muddled – or muddy, as he puts it in his soliloquy – as he. It is the human condition of which Hamlet is an exemplar.

Of course, if Hamlet had been alive in the 1920s, or had been an American in the 1950s or 60s, he would have gone or been sent to a psychoanalyst, who would likewise have tried to pluck out the heart of his mystery. He, the psychoanalyst, would have attributed his failure to the patient's psychological resistance, not to the inherent impossibility of the enterprise; if only Hamlet would continue the analysis long enough, the mystery would be plucked and Hamlet would stop dickering about and know exactly what to do.

In fact, Hamlet was psychoanalysed, and not just by any old psychoanalyst, but by one of Freud's first disciples, his first English-speaking follower and later hagiographer, Ernest Jones. Jones came to the conclusion – or perhaps I should say, started with the conclusion – that Hamlet was suffering from an unresolved Oedipus Complex. Hamlet's vacillation over what to do about Claudius arose not from his moral scruples, or from self-questioning and so forth, but from the fact that Claudius had usurped Gertrude's marriage bed, the bed that he had always wanted to occupy. He does not kill Claudius straight away, as easily he might, because to do so would reveal to him the desires that he must repress if he is not to become consciously aware of them. Moreover, he is ambivalent too about his father, who likewise occupied the bed that he always wanted (subconsciously, of course) to occupy. That is why he does not carry out his father's ghost's clear injunction to him. If he had done so, he would have realised that his feelings for his father were far less straightforwardly those of filial piety than those his conscious mind would like to have supposed.

Let us for a moment accept this preposterous and procrustean interpretation. The Oedipus Complex (unresolved in Hamlet's case) is at least as mysterious as the behaviour it is called upon to explain. If it is claimed that the Oedipus Complex is a brute fact of human nature – as at one time it *was* claimed, so that anthropologists went looking for it in the Trobriand Islanders – one might still ask how it arose, for no such explanation (that it was a brute fact of human nature) could be regarded as final, such that no further questions might be asked. And if some evolutionary explanation were found for it, that explanation would also not be final. If plucking out the heart of a mystery means finding the ultimate cause or nature of whatever it is that is mysterious to us, then – except for the religious – no heart of any mystery is ever plucked out. Some people are satisfied that this should be so, others not; but what seems to me certain is that Hamlet, and by extension all of humanity, *has* a mystery, a mystery whose heart, after many years of examination of patients, I am not any nearer myself to plucking out. Furthermore, I would not care to pluck it if I could.

CHAPTER SEVENTEEN

Nietzsche's 'Parable of the Madman' What happens when you unchain the Earth from the sun

Kenneth Francis

THE GERMAN ATHEIST Friedrich Nietzsche (1844-1900) was a miserable philosopher who was brutally honest about the horrors of existence without God. His message is also no friend of contemporary Secular Humanists, whose Happy Person Logo jumps for joy with unbridled optimism. Nietzsche, who would cringe at such Pollyanna folly, espoused nihilism, real atheism, despite being unliveable and void of any strong system.

Where Humanists espouse the virtues of *their* brand of equality, 'human rights' and compassion, Nietzsche abhorred such 'cowardly', 'weak values'. For him, survival of the fittest was the end goal for those striving to become the *ubermensch* (superman). Like Arthur Schopenhauer (1788-1860), whom he was influenced by, his writing style and ideas were both powerful and evocative.

The two German philosophers also shared a pessimistic view of humanity. When Nietzsche declared the 'death of God' at the end of the 19th century, he penned a parable outlining the ramifications for such a 'murder of all murderers'. It is likely Nietzsche was inspired either consciously or unconsciously by the Book of Ecclesiastes because he was well versed in the Bible. And the 'Parable of the Madman'[1] has echoes of the Preacher's teachings on a life without God.

> Nietzsche wrote: 'Have you not heard of that madman who lit a lantern in the bright morning hours, ran to the market place, and cried incessantly: "I seek God! I seek God!" - As many of those who did not believe in God were standing around just then, he provoked much laughter.'

Those who laugh at the 'Madman' are the village atheists, today's 'Intelligentsia' (the New Establishment). And it's possible the 'Madman' represents Nietzsche, who realises the nightmarish ramifications that awaited mankind after we murdered God.

> 'Has he got lost?' asked one. 'Did he lose his way like a child?' asked another. 'Or is he hiding? Is he afraid of us? Has he gone on a voyage? emigrated?' - Thus they yelled and laughed. The madman jumped into their midst and pierced them with his eyes. 'Whither is God?' he cried; 'I will tell you. We have killed him - you and I. All of us are his murderers. But how did we do this? How could we drink up the sea? Who gave us the sponge to wipe away the entire horizon? What were we doing when we unchained this earth from its sun? Whither is it moving now? Whither are we moving? Away from all suns? Are we not plunging continually? Backward, sideward, forward, in all directions? Is there still any up or down? Are we not straying, as through an infinite nothing? Do we not feel the breath of empty space? Has it not become colder? Is not night continually closing in on us? Do we not need to light lanterns in the morning? Do we hear nothing as yet of the noise of the gravediggers who are

---

1 Friedrich Nietzsche, 'The Gay Science' (1882, 1887).

burying God? Do we smell nothing as yet of the divine decomposition? Gods, too, decompose. God is dead. God remains dead. And we have killed him.'

Nearly two decades after Nietzsche wrote this, the first of the two Great Wars began, followed by more wars and nuclear explosions in Japan. This century-long conflict culminated in the biggest bloodbath ever, totalling over 100 million casualties. At no time throughout human history was such an horrific carnage carried out greater than in the 20th century.

Nietzsche had warned us about this. Every generation thought the world was becoming a worse place back then, but now the rot in the decline of civilization is certainly spreading with tremendous speed. With the horizon wiped away and the Earth unchained from the sun, parts of the 20th century certainly strayed through a finite nothing. And the early decades of the 21st century look like they could be outdoing Sodom and Gomorrah, as the Near and Far East is in conflict and the decadent (anti-)West is in moral decline.

Think about it: a depraved entertainment industry glorifying sex and riddled with satanic symbolism; websites promoting adultery; the promotion of all sexual deviant practices; a generation of brainwashed adults and students enslaved by media-inspired feelings; the relentless ongoing destruction of Christian civilization and war on the traditional family. One wonders when was the last time civilisation was run more disgustingly? Anthony Esolen, professor of Renaissance English Literature and the Development of Western Civilization at Providence College, said: 'What is the worst thing about living near an open sewer? It is not that you sicken at the stench of it every time you leave your front door. It is that the noisome vapours are so pervasive, and you have lived with them so long, you no longer notice it. What is the worst thing about living in the rubble of a civilization? It is not that you shed a tear for the noble churches and courts and town halls you once knew, as you recall years filled with religious services, parades, block parties, and all the bumptious folderol of an ordinary civic life. It is that you do not even suspect that such things existed.'[2] It is no accident that the 'sewer', which has been festering since the foot of the Cross, was subsequently ignited by the anti-Christian French Revolution and put into overdrive in the early-Sixties during the Sexual Revolution. Despot dictators are aware that a demoralised people are easier to control. Jesus said: 'Father, forgive them, for they know not what they do', (Luke 23:34). In such a crazy world, how do we find comfort in all of this madness?

> The Madman continues: 'How shall we comfort ourselves, the murderers of all murderers? What was holiest and mightiest of all that the world has yet owned has bled to death under our knives: who will wipe this blood off us? What water is there for us to clean ourselves? What festivals of atonement, what sacred games shall we have to invent? Is not the greatness of this deed too great for us? Must we ourselves not become gods simply to appear worthy of it? There has never been a greater deed; and whoever is born after us - for the sake of this deed he will belong to a higher history than all history hitherto.' Here the madman fell silent and looked again at his listeners; and they, too, were silent and stared at him in astonishment. At last he threw his lantern on the ground, and it broke into pieces and went out. 'I have come too early,' he said then; 'my time is not yet. This tremendous event is still on its way, still wandering; it has not yet reached the ears of men...'[3]

Unfortunately, many years ago it did reach the ears of men and women and continues today. Some strive to become God but are destined to failure both physically and spiritually. A world without God casts a dark shadow over our very origins, as we would be nothing more than evolved swamp goo. If Nietzsche truly understood the implications of Darwinism and its

---

2 Anthony Esolen, 'What Would Our Ancestors Think of Us?' *Crisis Magazine* (February 16, 2016).

3 Nietzsche, *Thus Spoke Zarathustra*, Part 4, 'The Magician'.

enslavement to the determinism of Nature, would he have encouraged us to choose and strive to become Supermen? And on Nietzsche's atheism, how could a molecular puppet even choose to reach the lofty heights of the Superman if freedom of the will is an illusion in a predetermined universe made only of matter?

Did he not understand that according to Darwinism, atoms do not develop morals and homosapiens can not choose to become either a superman or a weakling, in the same way a tree cannot choose to grow branches? Nietzsche once wrote a poem to an 'Unknown God,' crying out: 'Unknown one! Speak. What wilt thou, unknown-god?... Do come back with all thy tortures! To the last of all that are lonely, Oh, come back! And my heart's final flame - flares up for thee! Oh, come back, My unknown god! My pain! My last - happiness!' Nietzsche came across as an angry, bitter man. During the last decade of his life when he descended into madness, he sat quietly in bed with his mother occasionally by his bedside. Sometimes he would talk sporadically and recite passages from the Bible. Perhaps he suffered from a kind of God-vacuum as he sunk deeper and deeper into madness.

For the atheist David Hume, the God-vacuum could not be filled with games or amusement during his clouds of doubt. He wrote: 'Most fortunately it happens, that since reason is incapable of dispelling these clouds, nature herself suffices to that purpose, and cures me of the philosophical melancholy and delirium...'[4] Hume added: 'I dine, I play a game of backgammon, I converse...; and when after three or four hours' amusement, I would return to these speculations, they appear so cold, and strained, and ridiculous, that I cannot find in my heart to enter into them any farther'.

In 1898 and 1899, Nietzsche became partially paralysed after he suffered some strokes. This left him bedbound and he had great difficulty in speaking. In 1900, he contracted pneumonia and had another stroke. He died on August 25 of that year. Nietzsche's legacy on today's society is morally negative. That's not to say we should expect perfection in our day-to-day lives or in

---

4 Hume, 'A Treatise on Human Nature' (1, 4, 7).

those whom we admire.

Theodore Dalrymple wrote that no age is golden to those who live in it, and it is not often that men are more grateful for past progress than worried by current imperfections: 'Even so, our current age seems exceptional in the peculiarity of its unease. Never in human history have people lived such long and pain-free lives; never have so many people, and so high a proportion of people, had so much freedom to choose how to live, what goals to pursue and how to divert themselves. On the other hand, never have so many people felt anxious and depressed, and resorted to pills to ease their distress.'[5]

Yes, man is born unto trouble, as the sparks fly upwards.

---

5 Theodore Dalrymple, *Not With a Bang But a Whimper*, Preface, Monday Books (2009).

CHAPTER EIGHTEEN

Yeats' 'The Second Coming'
Theodore Dalrymple

The lines of this famous poem, written in the aftermath of that most catastrophic of all European catastrophes, the Great War, have been mined to an unequalled extent for titles to works by authors who seek to impart William Butler Yeats' gravitas to their work. While no detailed interpretation of a poem can be final or indubitably correct, few doubt that 'The Second Coming' is prophetic in a deeply pessimistic and, in the light of the years to follow, insightful, way.

Its most frequently-quoted lines will now probably never lose their salience:

The best lack all conviction, while the worst
Are full of passionate intensity.

Who, contemplating European history in the years that followed, or indeed our political and social situation now, would deny the resonance of these words? The passionate intensity of Lenin or Hitler can hardly be doubted, or that they were among the worst men ever to have directed a country's destiny. They were opposed by far better people whose decency seemed lukewarm and therefore lacking in conviction by comparison. Alas for humanity, conviction carries its own weight. How can a man so strident be wrong?

As for our own times, there is a shrillness to those who exude conviction that better, more balanced, people cannot match. For myself, I suspect that the shrillness indicates an underlying uncertainty or insecurity, as well as a desire to find a transcendent meaning to the existence of those who exude it. From where can this transcendence emerge, if not from a cause supposedly to produce a better world?

Religious belief has long been in decline: I suspect the shrillness of the Islamists arises from an awareness that if apostasy, conversion to other beliefs or free enquiry into such matters as the true history of the Koran were permitted, normalised and generalised, the centre could not hold, as it has not held in the case of Christianity, and mere anarchy, worse even than that at present, would be loosed both on the world and in individual psyches.

A comprehensive, true political religion such as Marxism (by true political religion, I mean, of course, not a religion that is true, but a political belief system that truly operates like a religion, albeit in an entirely secular sphere) seems to have lost its hold on the minds of western intellectuals, largely as a result of the downfall of the Soviet Union – however much Marxists may have protested that their brand of Marxism had nothing to do with the Soviet Union and vice versa.

The continuance of a tradition into which one was born is less and less able to supply transcendent meaning to modern people because we are all supposed to be entirely self-made or self-generating (personal development goes on until the day before death, and employees – including highly-qualified professionals – are still asked to produce personal development plans only weeks before their retirement, as if an eternity stretched before them).

In like fashion, the family no longer provides much sense of transcendence, any more than a kaleidoscope provides a fixed pattern for someone to copy. Its only constant is inconstancy. There is no felt link to the past or to the future. A family tradition means no more to people than does a national one, and indeed may come to seem more like a straitjacket, limiting or cramping the personal development of him who accepts it through lack of personality or character of his own.

While many, perhaps most, people still struggle to make a living commensurate with their desire to consume, it cannot in any real sense be called a struggle for survival, in as much as no one expects literally to starve. Mere survival, then, is not an achievement that can be an occasion for pride, and for those for whom material success is important, no success can be sufficient to satisfy.

What, then, is left for the intelligent, educated and reflective man who most likely works in a job that is physically undemanding and quite possibly intellectually and spiritually unsustaining? There remain causes, the attainment of whose ends is immediately followed by the adoption of other causes. The effect of past victories, which is usually equivocal, seldom gives rise to reflection, because the results are of less import than the struggle: it is more blessed to struggle than to win. And the reason it is more blessed to struggle than to win is that, so long as one is struggling, deeper questions of meaning and purpose are kept at bay. Shrillness that drowns out thought as white noise drowns our radio reception is the other indispensable means of avoiding reflection.

This is not to say that there are no good causes, of course; nor did the end of the Great War mean that there were any fewer of them. But if we examine the events of May, 1968 in France, for example, fifty years before I wrote this, we cannot help but see in that adolescent rising a thirst, simultaneously intense but also shallow, for transcendence. The students equated the regime under which they were living privileged lives with that of the Nazis, and the CRS with the SS. One of the most famous posters of the time showed de Gaulle's face as a mask, behind which was the true face of Hitler. Only deeply ignorant persons, complete egotists or moral imbeciles, could either have proposed such an equivalence or taken it seriously when proposed.

We may ask why they took it seriously. Surely there was a desire in it to suffer as the previous generation had suffered, or at least to be thought to have suffered as the previous generation suffered without really wishing to undergo the more uncomfortable aspects of that suffering. If there is one thing the cataclysm of the Second World War did, it was to answer what existence was for. It was for survival. Moreover, the events of that war were obviously of far greater significance than any one person's experience of them. Historical transcendence was in the air people breathed and in the exiguous food that they ate. The realities of ordinary prosperous social democratic life were too tame to satisfy the romanticism of spoilt youth: their passionate intensity was a screen for or protest against their own insignificance.

'The ceremony of innocence is drowned,' says Yeats: we can see this in the triumph, even within ourselves, of what has been called the 'hermeneutics of suspicion,' namely the idea that the hidden reality behind all human character, all social phenomena and all interactions, is something discreditable: a kind person is really a sadist, a mild-mannered person a power-seeker, and so forth. A policeman is not protecting the public, he is corruptly enforcing sectional interest; a teacher is not enlightening the young, he is instilling prejudices; a surgeon is not saving a life, he is making a living. There is, or can be, an element of truth in this, of course; but the hallmark of shrillness, the passionate intensity of which Yeats speaks, is that it takes the part for the whole, in order the better to give a simple meaning or purpose to existence.

Marx, Nietzsche and Freud were the three great masters of suspicion, the drowners of innocence, to which we have now added a fourth: Darwin, whose followers impress on us that we are only the envelopes, and that the real message is in our genes, that all our thoughts, strivings, reflections, are but epiphenomena to the deeper reality, the preservation and spread of the DNA within us. All four of these masters were irreligious, and all four reacted to the crisis of faith in which Europe as a whole was engulfed, of which they were both symptoms and causes. One thinks of Arnold's long, melancholy withdrawing roar.

But what will replace faith, the ceremony of innocence, after the apocalypse of the war? A perfectly just communist society? The Superman? Complete sexual freedom? Genetic engineering to make us perfect beings? Yeats is not so optimistic, if any of these visions of a better world can be called inviting:

> Surely some revelation is at hand:
> Surely the Second Coming is at hand.

The Second Coming, however, is not likely to usher in or restore a prelapsarian state. Yeats sees approaching:

> A shape with lion body and the head of a man,
> A gaze as blank and pitiless as the sun,
> Is moving its slow thighs, while all about it
> Reel shadows of the indignant desert birds.

A gaze as blank and pitiless as the sun: what could better describe the look of a Lenin, Hitler or Mao (and their like, of whom there have been disturbingly many) as they surveyed what they had wrought? Twenty centuries of stony sleep were vexed to nightmare by a rocking cradle, says Yeats: the Great War was the apotheosis or end-product of the long upward path of civilisation in which we deluded ourselves that we were progressing evenly, and now, as a result, we must ask:

> And what rough beast, its hour come round at last,
> Slouches towards Bethlehem to be born?

What terrible new Saviour will offer us his secular Salvation? Communism and racial purity were the first answer to take up the challenge. Islamism, full of passionate intensity, is the current contender, at least in some areas of the world: but it will not have the last word. A milder, totalitarian environmentalist paganism may yet step into the breach espied by Yeats. But who knows? Hope springs eternal, no doubt, but so do bad ideas. The human mind, like Nature, abhors a vacuum, and prefers vicious nonsense to nothing at all.

CHAPTER NINETEEN

Ibsen's *A Doll's House*
'*I married a monster from outer space*'
Kenneth Francis

O NE OF THE MOST POPULAR plays of all time is *A Doll's House* by Henrik Ibsen. And it's also one of the most performed plays of all time. Written in 1879, it premiered that year, four days before Christmas at the Royal Theatre in Copenhagen, Denmark. In its day, this play was shocking and radical.

Ibsen portrays the heroine of the play, Nora, to be someone pretending to be someone other than her 'true self'. Unlike all the women and men who wed and find married life at times difficult, Nora's having none of it. But consider what she does have: a big house, maids, three beautiful children, loving but occasionally patronising husband, Torvald, and comfortable surroundings.

However, she's had enough of being called endearing pet names by Torvald, who is a hard-working bank manager and regularly hands her big wads of cash while cuddling her. She's also annoyed that he's not 100 per cent perfect. It seems her standards for a husband are not just impossibly high, they're laughably impossible.

Most of all, Nora is furious because Torvald, although he's 'always been so kind to me', doesn't understand her (who fully understands his or her spouse?). She's also annoyed at him about a past secret debt and forged signature; all with good intentions. Furthermore, in this common, upper-middle-class marital situation, she not only doesn't 'exactly know what religion is' regarding morality, she cannot be her true self.

Led by her emotions, her standard of objective morality is zero, thus, of course, she *cannot* be her true self. Jesus said, 'if anyone would come after me, let him deny himself and take up his cross and follow me' (Matthew 16:24). But distancing herself from God has resulted in a disordered soul; and a troubled soul is a restless one.

She also doesn't believe 'any longer in wonderful things happening' (Join the club and welcome to the fallen world of Planet Earth). In the end, hoping for something wonderful to happen to 'improve' her situation, she slams the door on her husband and children and walks out on them in pursuit of her own 'liberation'. To repeat: she ruthlessly abandons her loving husband and three, young children.

Is Torvald really that bad or does Nora find bourgeois morality stifling? It's not like she married misogynist philosopher Arthur Schopenhauer or a monster from outer space. Or was she raised with amoral Enlightenment values? A really strong woman would surely have reprimanded her husband and communicated her displeasure by highlighting the spousal traits she abhors.

When psychoanalyst Sigmund Freud rhetorically asked, 'What do women really want?' the character Nora certainly comes to mind for any rational person who has seen *A Doll's House*. Only a lunatic could stand up and applaud a spoilt, rich woman abandoning her children. In fact, Freud's earliest work on psychoanalysis was on *Hedda Gabler*, the story of another self-absorbed, neurotic, suicidal, Ibsen heroine who craves freedom and authenticity.[1]

It was perhaps Gabler's mood changes and manifestations of hysteria that inspired the sex-obsessed Freud (a man who

1 Joseph Wood Krutch, 'Modernism in Modern Drama', Cornell University Press (1953). p. 11.

claimed that sexual restraint leads to neurosis and ill health). Fast-forward to the mid-20th century: if *Waiting For Godot* or *The Lesson* are fine examples of Theatre of the Absurd, then *A Doll's House* and subsequent radical Third-Wave Feminist plays spectacularly qualify for Theatre of the 'Oppressed'.

But despite the negative connotations of Ibsen's play from a Christian perspective, it is certainly not without artistic merit or entertainment value. However, some artistic works have consequences and *A Doll's House* is potentially a morally destructive work of fiction, whether wittingly or unwittingly. The same can be said for another much less artistic Third-Wave Feminist drama in modern times entitled, *The Vagina Monologues:*[2] a play that has been performed thousands of times in dozens of countries.

At some performances of this play, women are whipped into a frenzy of repeatedly shouting the slang 'C' word used for the female genitalia (it's hard to imagine Nora shouting this word at Torvald before she slammed the door).

If for many 19th century Europeans, *A Doll's House* was outrageous, then the 'Monologues' makes it seem tame in comparison. And one of the core messages about these plays is that women are responsible for nobody but themselves. How does that work out in marriage and relationships?: usually divorce or break-up. That's not to say that a man owns a woman, as if she's his slave. But, from the Christian worldview, two people of the opposite sex can only become one through the intimacy of marriage.

If Nora had studied the Bible, she would've understood we live in a fallen world, void of *ultimate* equality. The playwright and translator, Michael Meyer, said of *A Doll's House*, that the play's theme is 'the need of every individual to find out the kind of person he or she really is and to strive to become that person.'[3] (Psychopaths of the world rejoice!) However, Jesus said: ;Whoever finds his life will lose it, and whoever loses his life for my

---

2 Eve Ensler, 'The Vagina Monologues' (1996).

3 Michael Meyer, *Ibsen: A Biography*. Garden City (NY: Doubleday, 1971. Print.)

sake will find it.' (Matthew 10:39)

A statement about being true to oneself would bring great comfort to the world's dictators and evildoers. It would also give the green light to the millions of married men and women worldwide to commit adultery, tell lies, be lazy, selfish, abandon family, and a whole shopping list of flawed traits in the hearts and minds of us mortal fallen sinners. The Bible tells us: 'The heart is deceitful above all things and beyond cure. Who can understand it?' (Jeremiah 17.)

The problem with Nora, Hedda Gabler et all is their bondage to victimhood. And today, the 'Intelligentsia' constantly push the 'merits' of victimhood and oppression in a culture more confused than ever before. The writer, Eleanor Sharman, said that victim feminism taught her to see her body as inviolable and any action visited upon it as violence.

Eventually, she stopped going out as 'it wasn't worth the risk'. She said: 'It took me a long time to realise what had happened. Feminism had not empowered me to take on the world - it had not made me stronger, fiercer or tougher. Irony of ironies, it had turned me into someone who wore long skirts and stayed at home with her girlfriends. Even leaving the house became a minefield. What if a man whistled at me? What if someone looked me up and down? How was I supposed to deal with that? This fearmongering had turned me into a timid, stay-at-home, emotionally fragile bore.'[4]

She added that modern Feminism trains women to see sexism and victimhood in everything and makes women weaker. For all his seemingly 'patronizing' faults, Torvald was far from a typical male oppressor or primitive aggressive beast suffocating his little snowflake wife, Nora. What man has never felt like walking out on his spouse immediately after a long argument? And how many times in a fit of temper has a woman declared she hated her spouse, only to regret the fiery remark when the heat dies down?

Nora makes Torvald out to be some kind of condescend-

---

4 Eleanor Sharman, 'How I Became a Feminist Victim', *Spiked magazine*, February 10, 2016.

ing, intimidating villain. However, not all women striving for reasonable, fair equality see men as monsters. Author and former philosophy professor, Christina Hoff Sommers, says there's a distinction between equity Feminists and gender Feminists. Equity Feminists believe in equal rights, opportunity and reward for men and women. But Feminism has been taken over by gender Feminists, who wish to use the education system to transform male culture, according to Sommers.

Gender Feminists believe traditional female and male sex roles are invented by men to oppress women.[5] However, a 2006 study published in the UK's *Sunday Times* found women appear to be the main opponents of the advancement of women.[6] The study found that 'female rivalry in the workplace may sometimes be as important as sexism in holding back women's careers.' According to the study:

> Forget 'jobs for the boys', Women bosses are significantly more likely than men to discriminate against female employees, research has suggested. The study found that when presented with applications for promotion, women were more likely than men to assess the female candidate as less qualified than the male one. They were also prone to mark down women's prospects for promotion and to assess them as more controlling than men in their management style.

It seems a preponderance of women in managerial positions, in modern times, discriminate against other women, 'possibly because they like to be the only female manager or woman in the workplace.'

Life for men and women in relationships is a daily struggle

---

5 Christina Hoff Sommers, *Who Stole Feminism: How Women Have Betrayed Women*, Simon & Schuster (Revised Ed. 1995).

6 News item, December 31, 2006 UK *Sunday Times*, entitled, 'Office queen bees hold back women's careers,' the two authors, Roger Dobson and Will Iredale, report on a study of over 700 women by the Max Planck Institute of Human Development in Berlin; lead author: psychologist Rocio Garcia-Retamero.

and, although at times terrifying, can be highly rewarding and positive for society. No reasonable person is opposed to a rational Feminist movement that seeks fairness in higher education, property rights, fair positions in employment, and the right to vote. Any movement that seeks to protect the traditional family and to nurture love and kindness is welcomed.

However, it seems we've gone from a 19th century drama questioning the traditional rolls of men and women to a 21st century stage full of women saluting with the Communist raised right fist and endlessly talking about their vaginas. And this is viewed by many contemporary liberals as 'rational' and sophisticated? This new wave of gender Feminism went off the track when it started to demonize men and blame them for all the evils in human history, according to the Feminist icon Camille Paglia:

It's a neurotic world-view that was formulated in too many cases by women (including Gloria Steinem and Kate Millett) with troubled childhoods in unstable homes.

Paglia said her early role models, Amelia Earhart and Katharine Hepburn, were fierce individualists and competitors who liked and admired men and who never indulged in the tiresome, snippy rote male-bashing that we constantly hear from today's feminists.

I am an equal opportunity feminist who opposes special protections for women. What I am saying throughout my work is that girls who are indoctrinated to see men not as equals but as oppressors and rapists are condemned to remain in a permanently juvenile condition for life. They have surrendered their own personal agency to a poisonous creed that claims to empower women but has ended by infantilizing them. Similarly, boys will have no motivation to mature if their potential romantic partners remain emotionally insecure, fragile, and fearful, forever looking to parental proxies (like campus grievance committees or government regulators) to make the world safe for them.[7]

The message in *A Doll's House* surely looks like a smear on traditional family life and Christian values. Meanwhile, Scandinavia has become the most secular territory in the West. According to Mary Eberstadt, Senior Fellow at the Ethics and Public Policy Center in Washington DC, 'Who pioneered the unmarried Western family and its close ally, the welfare state (whose arguably critical role in secularization is also part of this picture)? Scandinavia.

'What is arguably the most atomized place in the Western world today, as measured by, say, the number of people who don't even live in a family at all? Scandinavia again.'[8]

It seems *A Doll's House* is a broken, Godless house. Nora might be a fictional heroine but she's no hero. The real heroes of this world are mothers who sacrifice everything for their children to grow up as decent, moral citizens. The abandonment of children has brought untold misery in this world where, over the past 40 years, it's not just the Nora's who are guilty, but also many men who walk out never to return home. But let's leave the last word to biochemist Roderick Kaine: 'Being a man or being a woman doesn't stop you from being an a*****e.'[9]

---

7 'Sam Dorman interviews Camilla Paglia', *The Washington Free Beacon* (May 15, 2017).

8 Interview with Mary Eberstadt, conducted by Gerald J. Russello, first published July 21, 2013 in *The University Bookman*, under the title, 'Faith and Family: A Two Way Street'.

9 Interview on Red Ice Radio, 'Smart and Sexy: Biological Differences Between Men and Women' (March 13, 2017).

CHAPTER TWENTY

Tolstoy's *The Death of Ivan Ilych*
Theodore Dalrymple

O UT OF THE WINDOW of my study in the house in which
I lived for more than ten years, I could see a rather
beautiful Victorian church which was not disused, exactly, but
which had large congregations only for weddings and funerals, perhaps like most churches these days. The funerals were
weekday affairs, and mostly of well-to-do people – or perhaps
I should say, of formerly well-to-to people. Important cars
parked round the church, and important people, dressed with
sober care, got out of them.

I watched the congregants emerging from the church: they
were clearly relieved that it was all over, that they could return
to their daily avocations. Their first act as they stepped out of
the church, many of them, was to look at their phones: perhaps
there had been important developments during the ceremony.
They looked as if they thought that death did not apply to them,
as if the dear departed had brought it on himself by carelessness
or some bad habit which, if avoided, rendered men immortal.

We tend to suppose that this embarrassment in the face
of death – above all, the congregants looked embarrassed – is
something new, a recent development in our increasingly secular society, in which the idea of a good death is (to coin a phrase)
dead, and in which death itself is regarded as anomalous. In-

deed, we are returning to the stage of the Azande, for whom all death was the result of malign witchcraft: only in our case, witchcraft has been replaced by medical negligence or error as the explanation of death. But *The Death of Ivan Ilyich*, which was first published in 1882, reminds us that the embarrassment caused by death is of longer date than we might suppose.

The first part of Tolstoy's novella – too long to be a short story and not long enough to be a novel – recounts the scene after the death, aged forty-five, of Ivan Ilyich Golovin, a respected examining magistrate who has always respected conventions and lived by the rules, so to speak. He had achieved quite a high position, but though his salary is good, he has always lived slightly above his means. To put on a good show for others has been important to him, always to be *comme il faut*.

After his death, his colleagues come to his funeral, but what they are thinking about is not him but how his death will affect their chances of promotion. If they had had mobile telephones to consult, they would have consulted them. One of them, his colleague Schwartz, winks at another of them, his childhood and closest friend, Pyotr Ivanovich, as if to say 'Ivan Ilyich has messed things up – not what you or I would have done.' I thought of my view of the church. And as for Ivan Ilyich's widow, Praskovya Fyodorovna, she soon reveals herself more concerned about the pension she will receive than mourning the death of her husband.

Having described with uncomfortable acuity the response of his circle to the death of Ivan Ilyich – uncomfortable because it is all too accurate and within our own experience – Tolstoy goes on to recount the last few months of Ivan Ilyich's life. Before he falls ill, Ivan Ilyich is a reasonably contented man. True, his marriage is far from happy, but he can divert himself from it with his work and his social evenings with friends and colleagues playing whist. In fact, playing whist is the joy of his life, and, like most men, he lives as if he will live forever.

While organising the decoration of his new flat, a task he considers of the utmost importance, he has a slight accident and bangs his side, which causes him pain. The pain, however, does not subside, as it should have done if it were only a bruise, but on the contrary nags at him and gets worse. Over the next three months, Ivan Ilyich grows more and more ill, weaker and weaker. From the description, he has a rapidly-progressing cancer, and it is a tribute to Tolstoy's astonishing accuracy to life that in fact people often do ascribe their subsequent cancers to a slight accident, which first brought their attention to the alien growth within them. In the United States there were indeed plaintiffs, supported by corrupt expert witnesses, who made bogus claims, sometimes successfully, that their cancers were caused by minor accidents some time before.

Before long, it is clear that Ivan Ilyich is dying. He knows it himself, and yet no one will be frank with him, not out of consideration for him, but out of consideration for themselves: they find it embarrassing to contemplate death. (As La Rochefoucauld says, one can stare long neither at the sun nor at death.) Everyone around him continues his or her life as if he were suffering from a minor inconvenience. The doctors whom he consults are no better: they disagree among themselves about what ails him, though each speaks in pompous circumlocutions that disguise his underlying ignorance and each prescribes uselessly elaborate diets and medicines (useless apart from morphine or opium which, if they do not cure him or even remove his pain entirely, at least blunt for a time his awareness of his situation). The doctors' self-important rituals serve no purpose except self-delusion, to prevent a clear awareness of their own impotence, just as the continued activities of Ivan Ilyich's household, friends and colleagues allow them to avoid thoughts of death, including those of their own mortality.

Thus an atmosphere of untruth envelops Ivan Ilyich that he finds more intolerable than the illness itself. It is agonising for him. His only relief from it is provided by Gerasim, a young peasant servant, who in a straightforward way tries to help his master because he knows that he is dying and says so. Here Tolstoy makes the contrast between his Europeanised and materially-advanced family and social circle, untruthful and unfeeling, and the peasant, kindly and truth-bearing. This, of course, accords with Tolstoy's Rousseau-like doctrine of the corrupting effects of wealth and his personal attempts to play the simple peasant, though really he remained the *grand seigneur*.

Just as painful as the atmosphere of lying that now surrounds him is Ivan Ilyich's survey of his own life, which he now realises had been always in pursuit of false gods. He has sought career advancement, a higher salary, respectability and the respect of colleagues who themselves have worshipped false gods. He has thought that appearances had to be kept up for the sake of others' opinions of him. That is why the furnishing of his flat was so important to him, despite (from Tolstoy's point of view) its obvious triviality and unimportance. It is of symbolic significance that the injury that he takes to be the cause of his cancer should have occurred while putting up curtains, not a cause worth dying for.

Tolstoy is too much the artist to make Ivan Ilyich a very bad man. He has never acted abominably, and the sins of his youth are watered-down versions of those that Tolstoy himself committed: thoughtless peccadilloes rather than anything calling for condign punishment. Far from being deeply evil, he is deeply ordinary, which is Tolstoy's point. Throughout his life, Ivan Ilyich has, like most people, merely followed a path almost laid down for him by his circumstances, without ever bothering to question what it was all for, whether it was right or whether there was a better way to live. He accepted the conventional values of those around him, toadying to his superiors and assuming a gravitas in court which in essence is no more than a charade or the playing of a part, the law itself (here Tolstoy is very Russian) being nothing more than the codification of injustice. Moreover, he has brought up his children to follow the same code; he wants his daughter to marry a lawyer who is a younger version of himself. It is not surprising, then, that while he lies dying, his wife and children go to the theatre to see Sarah Bernhardt act – the very acme of artistic falsity that Tolstoy excoriated in his *What Is Art?*

The last three days of Ivan Ilyich's life are terrible beyond description (except that Tolstoy has described them). He screams continually so that people even two rooms away cannot bear it. His agony is a compound of physical and spiritual pain. At the very end, however, there is a moment of redemption:

> Where was death? There was no fear whatsoever, because there was no death.

> Instead of death there was light.

> 'So this is it!' he said suddenly, out loud. 'Bliss!'

> All this happened in a single moment, and the meaning of that moment would not change.

The implication is that if Ivan Ilyich had followed the right path from the beginning, much suffering – both his own and that he inflicted on others – might have been avoided.

What are we to make of this? For me, the possible sudden redemption at the end of a life seems a double-edged sword. It offers hope, of course, but also, by giving the impression that nothing is irredeemable, promotes sin. There is surely evil that no repentance can redeem. And Tolstoy, like many men of giant ego, was not really capable of true religious belief or feeling. When Tolstoy found God, it was God that was honoured, not Tolstoy.

He, Tolstoy, also seems a little hard on ordinary humanity. This is not because he did not describe ordinary humans as they are: on the contrary, he did so with supreme accuracy. But it is the rigorist tone behind his descriptions that I find mildly unpleasant. The figure of Schwartz (perhaps it is not entirely a coincidence that he should have a German name) is held up to our disapprobation because, while Ivan Ilyich lies dead, he is thinking of his whist party. It is not that there are no people like Schwartz: on the contrary, most of mankind is like him. No doubt it is trivial to be thinking of whist in the presence of death: but what, really, is Schwartz supposed to do or to think? Is death to make Miss Havisham of us all? Is Schwartz to express a grief that he does not feel, or feel for long? That way humbug lies. Life must go on. After my death, the greengrocer must still open his doors and sell his cabbages.

CHAPTER TWENTY ONE

Joyce's 'The Dead'
A time to be born, a time to die
Kenneth Francis

'THE DEAD' is a short story by James Joyce from his book *Dubliners*, published in 1914. It is regarded as one of the greatest short stories in the English language. The crux of this essay focuses on the end of the story, as the dinner party is winding down and the guests leave.

The protagonist is a teacher called Gabriel Conroy who, with his wife Gretta, arrives late to a party on a winter's night in Dublin city, Ireland. During dinner, Gabriel begins a speech he has prepared, praising traditional Irish hospitality, observing that 'we are living in a skeptical...thought-tormented age', and referring to Aunt Kate, Aunt Julia and Mary Jane as the three graces.

The speech ends with a toast and a singalong. While preparing to leave the party, Gabriel finds his wife, looking sad and confused, standing at the top of the stairs. From another room, a dinner guest called Bartell D'Arcy, is singing 'The Lass of Aughrim'. Gabriel and Gretta leave the party and head to the hotel where they are staying.

As they arrive at the hotel, Gretta seems distant and melancholic. When Gabriel asks her what is wrong, she tells him she is thinking about that song, 'The Lass of Aughrim.' She says it reminds her of a man named Michael Furey, who had courted her many years ago. He used to sing that song for her and he died of an illness aged seventeen. As Gretta falls asleep, Gabriel is saddened and hurt that Gretta felt this way about another man. He becomes sad and reflects upon the countless dead in living people's lives, and observes that everyone he knows, himself included, will also die and be nothing more than a memory. As the story is ending, we are told that:

> His eyes moved to the chair over which she had thrown some of her clothes. A petticoat string dangled to the floor. One boot stood upright, its limp upper fallen down: the fellow of it lay upon its side. He wondered at his riot of emotions of an hour before. From what had it proceeded? From his aunt's supper, from his own foolish speech, from the wine and dancing, the merry-making when saying good-night in the hall, the pleasure of the walk along the river in the snow.

Gabriel feels like he's losing control over Gretta ('He longed to be master of her strange mood.'). But he's not consumed with jealously. In the Bible, God does not control us, despite having such power, but tells us that He's a jealous God (Exodus 20:4-5). Today, we view such a trait as selfish, suspicious, possessive, a 'green-eyed monster'. But the Old Testament word jealous derives from the word 'zeal'. And God is zealous about protecting what he loves and is precious to Him.Gabriel, who has a spark of the Divine, should feel the same way about Gretta, whom he loves dearly. Not to be hurt or jealous about someone you love would mean not to be consumed with love and passion. Jealously is not always the same as wanting to possessively control someone. God gives us free will to love or reject Him. Gabriel also has freedom of the will to leave Gretta, but her romantic feelings for another man, although deceased, plays havoc on his emotions.

His soul had approached that region where dwell the 'vast

hosts of the dead.' In one of his novels the author Somerset Maugham, wrote about the emotions of a character: 'He could not show his feelings. People told him he was unemotional: but he knew he was at the mercy of his emotions: an accidental kindness touched him so much that sometimes he did not venture to speak in order not to betray the unsteadiness of his will.'[1]

> Poor Aunt Julia! She, too, would soon be a shade with the shade of Patrick Morkan and his horse. He had caught that haggard look upon her face for a moment when she was singing 'Arrayed for the Bridal'. Soon, perhaps, he would be sitting in that same drawing-room, dressed in black, his silk hat on his knees. The blinds would be drawn down and Aunt Kate would be sitting beside him, crying and blowing her nose and telling him how Julia had died. He would cast about in his mind for some words that might console her, and would find only lame and useless ones. Yes, yes: that would happen very soon.

Just like Gabriel, all of us will one day have to face the grief of losing a loved one to death. Someone you meet today might pass away tomorrow. In John Huston's movie version of *The Dead*, the lead role is played by Donal McCann, one of Ireland's finest stage actors. I spoke to McCann many years ago while on a film shoot and, like Gabriel, he was quiet, deeply reflective and unassuming. At the time, he was also young, strong and solidly built. However, eight years after our chat, he died of pancreatic cancer, in 1999, at the relatively young age of 56.

But despite the pain and sorrow when the time of death arrives, for the Christian, we are not of this world and, on our deathbed, our decrepit and rotting body is in rehearsal for the bigger, eternal event. And even if our loved ones don't make it to Heaven, the Beatific Vision is the ultimate, self-communication of God with the physically deceased and spiritually reborn.

---

1 W. Somerset Maugham, *Of Human Bondage*, George H. Doran Company (1915).

This eternal, perfect salvation and vision of joy wipes away all forms of lamentation of those once loved. However, for the non-theist, the potentiality of grief and inevitability of death are inextricably linked to the terror of existence. The extinguishment of consciousness is philosophically, theistically and scientifically impossible, as mental states are not physical (try weighing or measuring love, joy, anger or logic). So where do our thoughts go? According to Christianity, Hell exists and those who are not paralyzed with fear by the unspeakable torments of it, obviously don't understand what it means. It means those who reject Christ will be separated in Hell for eternity.

In *Portrait of the Artist as a Young Man*, Joyce seems to have a good idea of the consequence of going to Hell. The protagonist, Stephen, lives in fear of Fr Arnall's fire-and-brimstone sermon. And what could be more terrifying than an eternal state of darkness, screaming, swearing, while all five senses are in enormous pain, never to end, in the company of your worst enemies and demons?

However, Scripture also tells us that there are degrees of punishment in Hell, just as there are degrees of reward in Heaven. 'That servant who knows his master's will and does not get ready or does not do what his master wants will be beaten with many blows. But the one who does not know and does things deserving punishment will be beaten with few blows' (Luke 12:47-48). For the metaphorically illiterate, these blows don't mean physical ones but degrees of sadness from separation from God. Gabriel's growing separation from Gretta has induced deep contemplation of his own, finite existence.

> The air of the room chilled his shoulders. He stretched himself cautiously along under the sheets and lay down beside his wife. One by one, they were all becoming shades. Better pass boldly into that other world, in the full glory of some passion, than fade and wither dismally with age.

It's important to understand the era in which *The Dead* is

based: Ireland, just before the Easter Rising, was allegedly a Catholic country, with a high mortality rate in both adults and children. It is also set around the time of the feast of the Epiphany (January 6, early 1900s), which celebrates the manifestation of Christ's divinity to the Magi.

But since the Enlightenment, the brand of Christianity taught in Ireland was (and still is) far from orthodox Scripture. Even Gabriel doesn't seem too religious. Ireland might have ostensibly looked like a Catholic country post-18th century, but it seems to be cryptically more anti-Christian. Why are so many 21st century Irish people repulsed by the legacy of the Church? From deviant, imposter 'priests' who infiltrated the Church, to corrupted, unsophisticated sermons on Scripture, it has reached the point where even the Godless BBC is asking 'is the pope a Catholic?'[2]

More than likely, Joyce, who was a cradle Catholic and educated by the Jesuits, was an atheist throughout his adult life. Writing in the *New York Times*, Jonathan Wolfe said when Edgar Allan Poe lived in a cottage in the Bronx, New York, 'he visited the Jesuits at a nearby college, now part of Fordham University. He was fond of the order, he told an acquaintance, because they :smoked, drank and played cards like gentlemen, and never said a word about religion'.[3]

One wonders how they taught or inspired Joyce, who also read the Godless Schopenhauer and listened to Wagner?[4] Much of his pessimism reflected in these two German writers can be seen in elements of Joyce's work, particularly 'A Painful Case', also featured in *Dubliners*. There's also the echoes of assonance in the prose in the final words of 'The Dead' and passages from Schopenhauer's *World as Will and Representation*. We might never know if Schopenhauer or Joyce passed boldly into that other world of God. (Joyce died a month short of this 59th birthday.)

---

2 'Is the Pope Catholic?' BBC World Service, *The Inquiry* (October 23, 2017).

3 *The New York Times*, 'New York Today' (January 19, 2017).

4 Wagner's *Tristan und Isolde*; Schopenhauer's *World as Will and Representation*

He thought of how she who lay beside him had locked in her heart for so many years that image of her lover's eyes when he had told her that he did not wish to live. Generous tears filled Gabriel's eyes. He had never felt like that himself towards any woman, but he knew that such a feeling must be love... His soul had approached that region where dwell the vast hosts of the dead. He was conscious of, but could not apprehend, their wayward and flickering existence. His own identity was fading out into a grey impalpable world: the solid world itself, which these dead had one time reared and lived in, was dissolving and dwindling. A few light taps upon the pane made him turn to the window. It had begun to snow again. He watched sleepily the flakes, silver and dark, falling obliquely against the lamplight. The time had come for him to set out on his journey westward. Yes, the newspapers were right: snow was general all over Ireland. It was falling on every part of the dark central plain, on the treeless hills, falling softly upon the Bog of Allen and, farther westward, softly falling into the dark mutinous Shannon waves. It was falling, too, upon every part of the lonely churchyard on the hill where Michael Furey lay buried. It lay thickly drifted on the crooked crosses and headstones, on the spears of the little gate, on the barren thorns. His soul swooned slowly as he heard the snow falling faintly through the universe and faintly falling, like the descent of their last end, upon all the living and the dead.

And in all of those graveyards, from the Bog of Allen to the dark Shannon waves, lie the remains of men, women and children, many of whom struggled with the wages of fear and terror of existence. In a Godless universe, the snow falls, the tide ebbs and flows, the pebbles draw back and fling, then begin again and again and again, the latter like that poignantly expressed in Arnold's classic poem 'Dover Beach'; while the rivers, seas and universe just keep rolling along, unaware, amoral and meaningless.

But with God, He will wipe every tear from our eyes. There will be no more death or mourning or crying or pain, for the old order of things has passed away. On this mountain, the Lord Almighty will destroy the burial sheet that enfolds all peoples, the blanket that covers all countries: 'He will swallow up death forever. The Sovereign Lord will wipe away the tears from all faces; he will remove his people's disgrace from all the earth' (Isaiah 25:6-8). – Upon the living, and the dead.

CHAPTER TWENTY-TWO

Matthew Arnold's 'Dover Beach'
Theodore Dalrymple

J UST AS IT IS FOOLISH to seek a precise date for the beginning of any social process, so it is foolish to seek for
the first realisation that it is taking place. But surely no one
would fail to cite Matthew Arnold's most famous poem, 'Dover
Beach', as a landmark in the decline of religious belief in western, or at least Anglo-Saxon, societies.

Matthew Arnold (1822 – 1888) was brought up in a strenu-
ous, not to say muscular, form of Anglicanism. He lost his faith
while still a comparatively young man, in his twenties, but he
never became the kind of militant atheist such as his contemporary, the first avowedly atheist Member of Parliament, Charles
Bradlaugh, who would stride on to the stage and challenge
God to strike him dead in five minutes (God bided His time,
it seems). Nor, unlike Nietzsche, did he imagine that the death
of God and religion would be a fine thing, ushering in the reign
of natural or Dionysian aristocrats? On the contrary, his poem
'Dover Beach', written around 1851 (and therefore at the high
point of Victorian optimism, for 1851 was the year of the Great
Exihibition, when it seemed as if material advance would save
the world), is full of regret and foreboding.

Later in his life, Arnold was read mainly for his religious
writings, or rather his writings that might be called theological.

He wanted to save Christianity, to many of whose teachings and traditions he remained attached, from the destruction wrought by then-contemporary philological and historical criticism that undermined a literal reading of the Bible. In his view, to make Christianity dependent on such a literal reading was danger- ous because it was so vulnerable to sceptical scholarship. Only a more metaphorical reading could save it; only if the Biblical account was never intended to be a kind of newspaper report of what happened could Christianity be salvaged from dissolution in people's minds (and with the advance of education, another of Arnold's preoccupations, unquestioning acceptance of dog- ma was likely to become ever more problematic).

Of course, there was a Charybdis to literalism's Scylla. If there were no historical facticity to the stories contained in the Bible, especially in the New Testament, Christianity would be- come a mere philosophy among others, with no transcendent validity or claims to special status. If the stories were to be read as mere metaphor, then it would be open to the supposed be- liever to take his metaphors from wherever else they seemed to him good. This was not a firm foundation on which to build or maintain a church: and in a sense, Christianity (it seems to me) has been wrestling with this dilemma ever since.

'Dover Beach' is a most melancholy poem: the mood is es- tablished from the first lines:

> The sea is calm to-night.
> The tide is full, the moon lies fair
> Upon the straits; - on the French coast the light
> Gleams and is gone; the cliffs of England stand,
> Glimmering and vast, out in the tranquil bay.
> Come to the window, sweet is the night-air!

There is clearly Romanticism at work in these lines. And, of course, melancholy is not an entirely unpleasant feeling: on the contrary, one can come to enjoy, almost wallow, in it. Moreover, there is a slightly illicit and unacknowledged pleasure to be had from Romantic agony and from the exhibition of one's existential dilemmas and doubts which go to demonstrate the depth of one's feeling and character. After all, only the shallow and unreflective go through life without them. There can be exhibitionism in one's religio-philosophical musings.

But I do not think it would be fair to accuse Matthew Arnold of this. Though he was a man of deep seriousness, he was by no means a scorner of the world's pleasures: he was witty, enjoyed company, particularly that of women, was something of a dandy, and he was an excellent father, though an unfortunate one, in as much as three of his sons died at the ages of 2, 14 and 19.

In 'Dover Beach', Arnold draws a parallel between the tide going out and religious faith, or rather the receding of religious faith:

> … from the long line of spray
> Where the sea meets the moon-blanch'd land,
> Listen! you hear the grating roar
> Of pebbles which the waves draw back, and fling,
> At their return, up the high strand,
> Begin, and cease, and then again begin,
> With tremulous cadence slow, and bring
> The eternal note of sadness in….

> The Sea of Faith
> Was once, too, at the full, and round earth's shore
> Lay like the folds of a bright girdle furl'd.
> But now I only hear
> Its melancholy, long, withdrawing roar,
> Retreating, to the breath
> Of the night-wind, down the vast edges drear
> And naked shingles of the world.

Without that faith, Man is left to face 'the naked shingles of the world' entirely on his own, with no other resources but his own. There is no meaning to life but what he chooses to give it, which some people find, or affect to find, exhilarating: Man as the measure of all things. But Arnold is not exhilarated or triumphal, but apprehensive: and history, I think, has shown him to be correct. It had frequently been urged against religion, not falsely, that it has often led to violent disputes, as if this were a decisive argument against it; but secularism, in its relatively brief career, has been, pro rata, even more murderous.

Left to our own devices in a vast and fundamentally meaningless universe, what is our comfort to be? Arnold seems to suggest in the next lines that it is our love for one another that can shield us:

> Ah, love, let us be true
> To one another! for the world, which seems
> To lie before us like a land of dreams,
> So various, so beautiful, so new,
> Hath really neither joy, nor love, nor light,
> Nor certitude, nor peace, nor help for pain…

But our love for one another is only a temporary shield, not only because – especially these days, now that there is neither sacrament nor contract nor sense of duty nor social disapproval to keep us together – our affections are mutable, but because we know that we shall not die at the same time and may face a prolonged period without one another. When the shield of love has gone, we are left defenceless again against a world in which there is neither joy, nor love, nor light, nor certitude, nor help for pain – unless, of course, it be resort to the equivalent of opiates (in the United States at the moment, not the equivalent of opiates, but opiates themselves).

What is the upshot of the melancholy, long withdrawing roar? Is it a population of happily mature and self-directed people, each finding his own meaning of life and pursuing it while being careful not to infringe anyone else's right to pursue his own meaning in life? I am afraid not, and Matthew Arnold was afraid not too: though I write with hindsight and he wrote with foresight. He ends the poem:

And we are here as on a darkling plain
Swept with confused alarms of struggle and flight,
Where ignorant armies clash by night.

Many ignorant armies have clashed by night since Arnold wrote those words, causing the deaths of millions (the Nigerian writer, Ken Saro-Wiwa, who was hanged for his political activism, titled his memoir of the Nigerian Civil War, *On a Darkling Plain*). Very few of those millions have died in the name of religious belief, but many have died in the name of a supposed secular salvation.

Of course, this leaves the essential problem untouched. If we accept that religious belief, provided it be not fanatical, is good for Man, that on the whole it conduces to good, or at least better, conduct, and that Man is much more at home in the world with it than without it, that it comforts him in the face of the inevitable existential limitations of human life (particularly death), the problem still remains: how to make it true for modern Man. This is the problem that Arnold faced, I think with clarity and honesty. He doubted doctrines, and certainly did not want them forced on people, *à la* ISIS, which in any case would have been counter-productive, at least in the long run. Furthermore, one cannot argue that something is true because it would be nice or comforting if it were true: the faith has to come first. But it has to be a faith that in turn can point to evidence.

Matthew Arnold never solved the dilemma for himself, but he put his finger on the problem with poignancy and with his poetic gift (which did not last long, however: the Muse left him, he said). Arnold later suggested that culture might serve as a substitute for religion, but even if there were some people for whom it might so serve, it certainly could not be for the great mass of Mankind, which has been left to its ever more extravagant distractions and membership of electronic communities of the self-absorbed.

CHAPTER TWENTY-THREE

Georges Arnaud's *The Wages of Fear* 'What was on the other side of that fence?' - 'Nothing'

Kenneth Francis

T HE 1953 CLASSIC FILM, *The Wages of Fear*, is not for those with a nervous disposition. This masterpiece of French-Italian cinema is based on a 1950 novel by Georges Arnaud. The French director Henri-Georges Clouzot co-wrote the screenplay for what was to become one of the most popular sub-titled films of all time. Boredom, dread, fear, alienation, corruption, anxiety, paranoia, misanthropy, greed, jealously, death and meaninglessness are all present in this nightmare of an existential thriller.

The plot is quite unusual: four European men, stuck in a hellhole South-American town, are hired to put out a fire in an oil rig some 300 miles away. The location of the inferno is over a mountain and through unpaved, treacherous, pot-holed dirt roads. The main characters are two Frenchmen, a Dutchman and an Italian. The plan is for the men to drive two trucks loaded with two tonnes of nitroglycerine to the oil field in order to blow up the blaze, thus extinguishing the massive fire. The trucks have to be driven at a snail's pace in order to avoid a fatal disaster with the delicate explosives.

The Wages of Fear is seriously explosive in its bleak message. It is infused with nihilistic philosophy and the ideas of Camus and Sartre. The atheist Existentialists believed that there is no God and humans are 'condemned to be free'. This philosophy is irrational as without God there is no such thing as freedom of the will. If everything is permissible, then torturing Camus and Sartre would be no different to nurturing the pair and treating them with kindness.

In Sartre's play, *No Exit*, the final lines in Hell are: 'Well, let's get on with it.' And that's the attitude of the four men in *Wages of Fear*. Sartre also writes about the 'nausea' of existence. And in Camus' novel *The Stranger*, the protagonist discovers that there is no meaning in life and no God to give it.

But back to the film: brutally unsentimental and cruel, existential angst and death hovers over the characters like a wake of vultures. In the opening scene of the film, a village child tortures what appear to be several cockroaches tied together on the ground. Cruelty is featured throughout most of Clouzot's films. Like his fellow Catholic maverick director, Alfred Hitchcock, to whom he was compared, betrayal, deception, murder and lust are typical sins par for the course in a Clouzot story.

As the children torture little creatures, a town riddled with gypsies, tramps, thieves, rogues and peasants bakes daily in the sun. A cruel, bored man sits outside a local saloon throwing stones at a dog on the street. While the dog yelps, the flies buzz and the financially broke, motley foursome dream of escape.

One of the characters, a cold-hearted, playboy-type drifter called Mario, hangs around the bar while the pretty maid Linda yearns for his attention, scrubbing the floor at his feet. After the men apply to the 'greedy' American oil company for the 300-mile potential-suicide mission, they set out on their journey to reap their $2,000-a-head reward to freedom.

Every jolt and bump on their journey is a reminder of instant death by incineration. It also reminds us of our own life journeys in this fallen world and how death can take us any second, minute, hour or day. These men had overcome other obstacles on their journey to the blaze but a bump on the road blows one of the trucks and two men to smithereens.

In a world without God, every move is anticipated with existential terror. When the second truck arrives at the scene of the explosion, the character, former gangster Jo, badly injures his leg when the vehicle gets stuck in a bog created by the blast and subsequent severed oil line. Drenched from head to foot in oil, he later lies dying in the cab beside his Parisian workmate.

He starts to reminisce and asks the cold, sarcastic Mario about a shop in Paris that they both knew many years ago. He says: 'You remember that fence? What was on the other side?' Mario replies: 'Nothing. A vacant lot.' Seconds later, Jo utters his last words before dying: 'Nothing!' Mario drives on and eventually delivers the nitroglycerine.

Driving back to the village at speed, swerving along the way, he looks ecstatic having escaped death, as a Strauss waltz plays on the radio. Back in the village, the homecoming party is in full preparation, with Linda and the villagers dancing in the Cantina. Meanwhile, as Mario speeds down the mountain in a reckless fashion, Linda collapses on the floor. This scene is juxtaposed with Mario's truck skidding through a guard-rail and over the rock, plunging Mario to his death.

In an era of Hollywood happy endings, *The Wages of Fear's* final scene was unusual. It is also what we'll all have to face one day: death. But in this Theatre-of-the-Absurd landscape without God, the blood, sweat and tears of Mario's journey were ultimately in vain. Everything becomes undone. And who cares?

According to Naturalism, these wet robots made of meat are not moral agents. But surely our free will and own personal agency is obvious? But if the laws of physics trump everything, the conclusions are horrifically shocking. It means that whatever we do is determined. Hyenas, crocodiles and tigers have no regrets, so why should moist machines like us have them?

Moral values and duties become expressions of personal taste. In Darwinism, we become the by-products of socio-biological evolution and conditioning. Any concept of moral obligation is delusional. Moral indignation becomes irrational. (Are zebras morally outraged at their brutal treatment by hungry lions? Is being eaten alive a scandal and inconvenience to the survival of their species?) Mario certainly has a lion's heart. He looked upon Jo's death as an inconvenience. It's almost as if the characters all secretly hate each other.

Jesus said, if the world hates you, remember that it hated me first. Before dying, Jo cries out, 'Nothing!' Without Christ, ultimately there is nothing. 'All people are like grass, and all their glory is like the flowers of the field; the grass withers and the flowers fall.' (1 Peter 1:24). In Schopenhauer's universe, Mario lies dead at the bottom of a rock being devoured by hungry creatures of the forest, his atoms recycled on their final journey toward the heat death of the universe.

> The fate of the sons of men and the fate of beasts is the same. As one dies so dies the other; indeed, they all have the same breath and there is no advantage for man over beast, for all is vanity. All go to the same place. All come from the dust and all return to the dust (Eccles.3:19-20).

The 'greedy' oil company gets to keep Mario's paycheque. Without God, what did these men gain from all their labours at which they toil under the sun: death? More men will come and go, but the sun rises on the same hellhole village they left and the sun sets, and hurries back to where it rises again and again and again. 'All things are wearisome, more than one can say.'

For the four men, everything was meaningless, a chasing after the wind; nothing was gained under the sun (Eccles.2:11)... *The Wages of Fear* is a parable of life without God. We travel on our journey through life walking on eggshells, trying to avoid 'bumps' along the way. Some of us are metaphorically 'blown up' by obstacles along the road; others live a little longer before 'falling off the cliff'. In the end, without God, it is all for nothing.

It's possible the younger Clouzot was an atheist when he wrote the screenplay for *Wages of Fear*, but he converted to Catholicism in the early 1960s. Did he initially intend to show a deistic, demon God looking down at us insects, tied together in this torturous life? Or is this deist God disgusted with His creation, as He backs off while we wreak moral havoc on the Earth?

In a perfect world, *The Wages of Fear* would never work at inspiring us to reflect about the ultimate meaning of our lives. Only in a life where suffering exists are we drawn closer to God. Think about it: a hypothetical movie called *The Wages of Pleasure*, where four handsome men in two Mercedes-Benz cars deliver body oils, perfumes and soaps to a coterie of young beautiful women in a Playboy Mansion somewhere nearby on a paradise beach. A hollow, bland movie devoid of tension, suspense, action, suffering and fear. This spectacle of tacky boredom with transient cheap thrills would never work. It seems that when Gottfried Leibniz said we inhabit the best of all possible worlds, he might have been on to something.